THE GIANTS' SHOULDERS

COLLECTED WISDOM FROM THE BALI GSS CONFERENCE 2024

First published 2024 by Indie Experts

Published Produced by Indie Experts
indieexperts.com.au

Indie Experts wish to acknowledge the contribution of the esteemed
Speakers and Authors that have contributed towards the content of this book:
Antoni Lacinai, Brad Hauck, Kate Delaney, Dixie Carlton, Dave Greenberg,
Bronwyn Reid, Lindsay Adams, Leila Kubesch, Brad Shorkend.

Cover design and typesetting by
Ammie Christiansen, Fast Forward Design
Typeset in 11pt Minion Pro

ISBN
Printed: 978-1-7386102-7-3
eBook: 978-1-7386102-6-6

Disclaimer:
Every effort has been made to ensure this book is as accurate and complete
as possible, however they may be errors both typographical and in content.
The authors and the publisher shall not be held liable or responsible to any
person or entity with respect to any loss or damage caused or alleged to have
been caused directly or indirectly by the information contained in this book.

BY THE SPEAKERS, FOR THE SPEAKERS

THE GIANTS' SHOULDERS

COLLECTED WISDOM FROM THE BALI GSS CONFERENCE 2024

iX
indieXperts
PUBLISHING & AUTHOR SERVICES

Introduction

If you sat down with any group of professional speakers who have reached the levels that those in this book are at, you'd find they would all want to share a range of special wisdom gleaned from years developing their expertise and getting that content from inside their heads, and out into their markets. Reaching audiences, readers, and clients who want to know more about what they have to share is what drives every professional speaker. However, when I contemplated creating this book project, it was with one thing in mind: these speakers needed to share what's relevant with other professional speakers.

This is not a book about leadership, marketing, motivation, or any of the topics covered at any other conference around the world. Instead, this is a collection of the wisdom being shared at the Global Speakers Federation biennial summit. It is by speakers, for speakers.

Presented in three main areas – The Stage, The Planning, and The Service – this content is a handy collection of "if you knew then what you know now" information you can use right now to make your speaking business better.

There's outstanding advice about publicity, selling and value-adding from and beyond the stage, how to plan for and thrive through a major disruption to your business, and the value of giving back to the industry in which you wish to achieve a level of mastery. Oh, and so much more. *What you'll find in here has been curated and shared with **you** in mind.*

Please feel free to reach out to those who have taken the time to write these essays. Invite them to hang out, share a ride to the airport, speak at your next chapter event or conference, or recommend them to present at one you're speaking at.

Please enjoy this book, and remember to leave a review or reach out if you'd like to be considered for participation in the next edition two years from now.

Be unstoppable,

Dixie Maria Carlton

CPO: Indie Experts Publishing and Author Services
www.indieexpertspublishing.com

Contents

THE STAGE

Chapter 1:

Nine Memory Hacks for Your Audience

Antoni Lacinai — Sweden

"You cannot act on what you don't remember."

I got this quote a few years back from a book about memory. The irony is that I can't remember which book, so I can't give the author proper credit. Nevertheless, the quote is a gem for us speakers. You see, I believe that our role, every time we are on a stage, is to facilitate change. Mentally, spiritually, physically.

Change means movement, and movement means action. If I share something in a keynote or lecture, and you forget it the minute you leave the venue, how can I expect you to change? Sometimes we are more interested in looking good, forgetting that we can share something actually transformative to another person. This has happened to me more times than I want to admit, and I am sure it happens to you too. Sometimes, even if you do a great job, or so you thought, your message doesn't stick. It's frustrating.

I remember way back when I still had a "normal" job as a marketer at Ericsson, a global telecom company. I was walking down a street in Stockholm, lost in my own thoughts, probably late to a meeting. It was early spring, and the sun was shining. On the other side of the street, I noticed a man staring at me. Like a heat-seeking missile, he crossed the street to intercept me. At first, I felt uncomfortable. My inner radar released stress hormones and prepared me for fight or flight. But I calmed down a bit when I saw this stranger's happy face. He seemed genuinely happy to see me.

"It's you! It's you!" he half shouted.

"It's me. It's me," I responded. *"Who are you?"*

"Ah, you don't know me, but we are colleagues. I was in the audience when you presented in Florida last year."

The fact that I didn't know him wasn't a mystery. In Stockholm alone, I had more than 15,000 colleagues. I remembered the event clearly. I was part of a market launch team, and I had just taken on a role working with competitor analyses. My presentation at the conference was about helping each other by sharing what we knew about our competition. The title was "If only Ericsson knew what Ericsson knows." And my call to action was for the people in the audience to connect and share their insights with me. Regrettably, I didn't get any traction from them after the event. It bothered me, and I couldn't put my finger on why. But working in a large corporation, you quickly get busy by just attending more meetings, so I had mentally put it aside.

The man continued. *"I saw you rock the stage. You were awesome, man!"*

I smiled and immediately grew an inch. *"Thank you,"* I said, remembering the massive applause I got.

Then came the blow. He said, *"I don't remember anything you said, but you were awesome!"*

That inch I just grew: gone. I muttered another thank you, and after a quick chat, I went on my way. But that encounter planted a seed of doubt in me. I still remember it as a pivotal moment where my life changed, ever so slightly. I realized that it wasn't enough to get ovations and applauds. It was too… shallow. All talk, no action. I needed to up my game.

Think about the word "presentation". The first part of that word is "present". You are giving a present-ation. A great present has beautiful gift-wrapping, and inside is content that is appreciated. What I gave the audience in Florida was the gift-wrapping. Great energy, great body language, great tonality. But inside the box was only air. No relevance, no value, no content.

I am not saying that the gift-wrapping is unimportant. If you are a wine collector and I brought you wine wrapped in newspaper previously used in the fish market that gave you gag reflexes from the stench of rotten fish, chances are you wouldn't bother to unwrap it to find out what was inside. The way you present matters. But if that is all your audience remembers, you will not facilitate change. Your personal brand might get a boost, and perhaps your minutes on stage gave some of them relief from their daily worries, but that's it.

Non- Verbal Communication

I believe we can do better. And it starts with them remembering at least some important messages we shared.

"I've learned that people will forget what you said, people will forget what you did, but people will never forget how you made them feel." — Maya Angelo

I think we can all agree that this is a beautiful piece of wisdom. The problem is that for you as a speaker, this is not helpful. It is not enough. It is, in fact, useless. By realizing this, you can take on the challenge and create and deliver something memorable. You can facilitate change. You can be a change maker. You don't have to experience the whole "I don't remember anything you said but you were awesome…" thing (which at least is better than "I don't remember anything you said except you sucked").

So, what can you do to be more memorable, and specifically to make your content stand out? In the rest of this chapter, you will get nine concrete hacks on how to create and deliver memorable content. You probably already do most, if not all, of them. Compare yourself with 99 per cent of any business presentation and you will excel. Pat yourself on the shoulder and check the box. Then ask yourself how you can hone your skills even more. If you notice there is something you haven't tried, then I challenge you to test it – more than once. If you fail the first time, don't give up. The advice is solid. You might just need to execute it better.

The Nine Steps:

1. Once Upon a Time

There is no single method, no technique as powerful, as storytelling. You will not only reach out, but you will also reach in. It is borderline magic!

Imagine that everybody has an intellectual bouncer in their brains. You start showing slide after slide with text, text, text, plus some stats, etc. The bouncer can easily stop any of that from entering the brain, claiming that *"This brain doesn't believe that."* But if you share a story, the bouncer will be utterly confused and say, *"I don't know what to do with this. Here, let me open the door. Step inside. Go and find the CEO, located somewhere around the limbic systems… yes, right there where it says 'emotions'. Talk to my boss instead of me."* Brains cannot refuse to listen.

It is part of our DNA to sit around a fireplace and share stories. You simply must share stories, examples, anecdotes, etc. And the better you are at telling your stories, the more the audience will enjoy and remember them.

Apart from the basic ingredients of

- a time
- a place
- a person
- a problem
- a solution

you will add senses, so that your audience can imagine and experience what you say. Can you make them see what you see, hear what you hear, feel what you feel? It will help them "be inside" your story.

If you also act out with dialogue and "become" the different people in the story, you increase energy even more. People remember more when they feel a heightened state of energy, so this will also improve their recall.

A word of warning: A story without any relevant lesson or connecting insight is just entertainment. A lesson without a story is often boring. Together, though... *wow!*

2. "Honey...aaa Sugar Sugar"

Charismatic people use 50 per cent more metaphors than the average Joe. Charismatic people also use storytelling, the power of three, and basically every other memory hack I will share with you. On top of that, they show courage and set high goals, they show empathy, and they use their body language as well as their voice. They ask rhetorical questions (many of these skills also trigger memory, so regard them as bonus hacks). But I digress. Let's explore why metaphor is so valuable.

A metaphor takes anything abstract, unknown or complicated into familiar and concrete territory. Who can really grasp 5G? I, who spent eight years in the telecom industry before leaving in 2006 to be a speaker and coach, cannot explain it in any technical terms. Even if I could, you wouldn't get it. But if I say that 5G is a superfast highway compared to 4G, which is a country road, and 3G, which is more of a gravel path, you get the concept. Fast. That's probably all you need to know, unless you are a propeller head (see? a metaphor for tech geek) and a telecom nerd.

An analogy is the same as a metaphor but with one difference. You start an analogy saying "It's like..." They both do the trick and help your audience understand what you say, thereby increasing the chance of remembering your message by infinity compared to not grasping any meaning at all.

If a picture paints a thousand words, a metaphor paints a thousand pictures. —Michael Henderson

3. THREE is the Magic Number

Think about all the stories and fairytales you heard when you were growing up. A surprising number of them include the magical power of three.

- How many wishes did Aladdin get from the genie?
- How many bears did Goldilocks encounter?
- How many musketeers are there in the classical story from France? (Actually, there were four. But we remember the "Three Musketeers", don't we?)

I can go on with other triads. The Father, the Son, and the Holy Ghost. Or Brahman, Vishnu and Krishna?

It seems that as soon as we go above three messages, we put a cognitive overload on people. I am guilty of this all the time, when I share 7 motivational boosters, 9 steps for great feedback, or 20 communication insights. Not to mention "9 memory hacks"... But I also work hard to give them in chunks of threes whenever I can. For instance, the three communicative superpowers that I constantly preach about are **Energy** (so people believe that you believe), **Empathy** (so they feel that you get them), and **Clarity** (so they get you). By the way, this whole chapter is – almost – exclusively about the superpower of Clarity. Except for tip number 5.

One of my sons is studying mathematics at university. When he was a very young boy, he once counted something. I still remember him saying, *"One, two, three ...many."*)

Say one thing and give three examples.

Say two things – like you will see in bullet point number 8.

Or say three things – but not more.

4. Fill in the _____

Which word comes next?

- Faith, hope and _____

- Blood, sweat and _____

- Sex, drugs and _____

If you didn't know the answer, the words are *love, tears, and rock'n'roll*. Most people know at least one or two of them. The trick here is that your brain naturally supplies the word that completes the trio. It's the same with your audience. When they get it right, or when you share the correct answer, they are rewarded with a dopamine rush. It feels good. It also makes them remember that content better. So how can you create a mantra of three things that sit together within your own presentation or topic?

For example – Start, middle, end; red, yellow, green (stop–pause–go); hard, medium, soft.

5. You Had Me at Hello

When Tom Cruise stands there in front of Renee Zellweger in the movie *Jerry McGuire*, his character is overwhelmed by emotion when he explains his true passion and how he has been an idiot. Renee's character waits and then delivers the epic line, *"You had me at hello."* Not only is it an awesome one-liner (another bonus hack for jogging memory), but it shows that passion beats logic and helps us remember more since we are now emotionally invested. I mentioned this briefly in hack #1, where I said that if you are acting out your story, then you will be more energetic.

By the way – Energy is one of the three superpowers of communication!

The cool thing is that we have these mirror neurons in our brains. If you smile, I smile. If I see you fall and hurt your knee, the same areas that light up in your brain will light up in my brain too. By demonstrating your passion for your topic – by emphasising what's important, using strong gestures and facial expressions – you will get people to remember more than if you have a poker face and restrained body language. Unless you are a comedian.

6. Do the Yin and Yang Dance

Polarities create tension. I was at a European speaker summit, where I shared views on how to make your speech more personal. On one side of the stage, I had a flip chart where I drew an angry face. On the other side, I had a flip chart where I drew a happy face. That was it. Now I could approach the different sides depending on the examples I shared.

When using polarities, the audience gets involved with their own questioning of is it right or left? Right or wrong? Black or white? Yes or no? Good or bad? This makes people take a stand. They become activated, searching for the right answer. This increases their chance of remembering the opposites – the polarities – you present.

7. Bring the Popcorn

Using props instead of PowerPoint is often refreshing, and used right they will act as a trigger; when that trigger is released, your audience will suddenly remember what you said. I often use a bag of microwave popcorn in my speeches when I talk about employee engagement. I do a whole act on why people are like the corns in the back, how it takes time and energy to make them pop, and how some refuse to pop. I tell them to think about their own situation as a leader or colleague the next time they make some popcorn. This will trigger their memory.

I am playing with a similar idea of using coffee filters while talking about either core values or about leaving negativity behind when you enter your workplace. (I have some work to do before getting it right.) If I succeed, every time they bring out a new filter, chances are high that they will remember what I talked about. I know that some of you have giveaways. It's not necessarily the same as a prop within a keynote, but it can still aid their memory, done right.

What can you use as props? The legendary speaker Tim Gard, CSP CPAE, does this extremely funny piece where he has three chairs on the stage, and talks about how he ends up in the middle seat. It is brilliant! He could have done it without the chairs, but they add to the experience. I, too, sometimes use a chair when I speak about coming home after being held at gunpoint. The chair symbolizes the bedside and how I sat down on the bed, unable to lie down, because I suddenly realized that I had just escaped death...

8. SURPRISE!!!

Consider what would happen if you did something truly unexpected.

- What if you brought a real brain or a dead chicken to the stage when you talked about consciousness and neuroscience?

- What if you created a stunning painting or sketch of your topic while speaking?

- What if you suddenly SHOUTED OUT LOUD, danced, or stripped to reveal a costume?

- What if you shared a fact that was mind blowing, or an idea worth spreading?

I guarantee they will remember it. Most people don't use the element of surprise. I sometimes struggle with this in my communication keynotes, getting responses like *"That was great! And so good to be reminded..."*, meaning that I offered nothing new, even if I packaged it differently. I have worked quite a lot to find some elements of surprise, with the hope they will also say, *"I hadn't thought of it like that,"* or *"I didn't know this. Now I must..."*

People do like some predictability. Total chaos will exhaust them. If they had an inner traffic light, you want that light to turn green, so that they are at ease and open to your ideas. But don't underestimate the power of variation and dynamics. People also like surprises. Find a nice balance where they get both. What surprises them will stand out – just make sure it is the right kind of surprise, and not the ones you get in the next hack...

9. I would do anything for love, but I won't do that.

Here is what not to do: If you go for surprises, don't do a gimmick that distracts the focus from your content and lacks any relevance to what you will say. It's cheap, and it is stupid.

Here are two examples I have heard from friends:

1. They: *"I remember my first day at university. The professor came up on stage and accidentally dropped all his papers on the floor. We all gasped. Then he picked them up and started his lecture. I later found out that this was a gimmick. It was so funny. I still remember it!"*

   Me: *"But do you remember what he talked about?"*

   They: *"No..."*

2. They: *"It was so funny. I saw this speaker. She promised us that she would show a picture of herself naked at the end of the speech. And she did. She showed us a picture of herself as a two-year-old. Naked! It was hilarious!"*

   Me: *"But do you remember what she talked about?"*

   They: *"No..."*

I once witnessed a woman who ran an ad agency giving a brand message presentation. She decided it was a good idea to have angel wings attached to her clothes. She also hired an artist who created a painting behind her – none of which had anything to do with brand messages. Nothing at all. I have no idea what she said. But I do remember the angel wings...

In summary

- People cannot act on what they don't remember!
- If you want to be a change maker, you must reach both their hearts and minds.
- Whatever you say or do should strengthen your message and help the audience remember the right things.

You got this!

Thanks for reading my mind

Antoni

About Antoni Lacinai

The Workplace Motivation and Communication Expert

Antoni Lacinai left copororate life in 2006 to focus on emcee and presentation skills training, before moving into the keynoting speaking. Today, he inspires with strategies for super-engaged teams through top-notch communication and empathy. Antoni is giving keynotes and trainings around the world. Even though he doesn't enjoy the actual traveling part of running between terminals, stressed out and anxious, he still feels it is worth it once he meets his clients and audience. Antoni has authored/co-written 14 books. He is a regular columnist in various magazines and is often interviewed on Swedish national TV.

Antoni lives in Sweden where he loves to create simple illustrations for his keynotes, even simpler songs for his friends, and not simple enough business blueprints for his customers.

www.antonilacinai.com

Chapter 2:

Seven Ways to Make Massive Profits from the Stage

Brad Hauck — Australia

Are you ready to turn your stage presence into a profitable venture? Whether you're a seasoned speaker or you're just starting out, there are numerous ways to monetise your time on stage effectively. These methods – from selling training courses to creating recurring services – offer opportunities for you to engage your audience, deliver incredible value, and generate income.

To sell from the stage, you need to show your audience that you're the expert they need to grow their business. Your main goal is to connect with them personally, building trust and credibility. This means not just sharing great content but also knowing their needs and problems. Use your time on stage to show the value of what you know and how it can help them. Be clear, confident, and excited by your topic. Use a mixture of subtle though strong calls to action to encourage them to buy. Then you can move smoothly from teaching and entertaining to making sales and earning money.

It's a skill well worth perfecting.

1. Selling Training Courses

This is a highly profitable option. People often overcomplicate the process, but it's essential to keep it simple. You already know from attending training courses that simplicity makes the material more understandable. You can offer these courses in various formats. Live sessions in a physical room are effective and engaging, allowing direct interaction with participants. Alternatively, live online courses are increasingly popular, reaching a broader audience without any geographic limitations. Recorded courses offer even more flexibility. You can sell them as on-demand content, allowing people to start whenever they like, or you can organise participants into cohorts. This means they go through the course together, which creates a sense of community and shared learning. The options are adaptable to your style and audience.

Realistically, the primary costs in producing a training course are your preparation time, advertising, and the hosting for your website or course. You might also need streaming software, depending on your preferred delivery method. Fortunately, many affordable options are available for both streaming and recording video, and many platforms like Thinkific and Systeme have this built in.

There are many budget-friendly software options for live streaming of online training. Zoom, for instance, costs around USD$20 a month and offers reliable service. Other options great for engaging with your audience without significant investment are Facebook Live and LinkedIn Live. The key is to choose an option that ensures you can deliver your course effectively without breaking the bank.

There are also free options that can be integrated with various software platforms. You can host your course on numerous platforms, each offering unique benefits. Personally, I favour Thinkific and Heights Platform. Lately, I've been using Dot.io for setting up funnels and other tasks.

For those looking for deals, joining the AppSumo mailing list is a great strategy. AppSumo frequently offers course software at discounted rates. You might worry about the longevity of these deals, but I can assure you that many of them are reliable. For example, I purchased the Heights Platform through AppSumo a few years ago, and it's still functioning well. There are plenty of robust options available, so don't hesitate to explore and find the right fit for your needs. In fact, many of these platforms use initial deals as a stepping stone for growth, allowing you to snag some excellent bargains. It's a smart strategy, even if you use the software for only a few years before upgrading to a bigger platform as your revenue increases.

When creating a course, I recommend running it live twice, either online or in person. During these trial runs, pay close attention to any issues that arise. Look out for moments where participants seem confused or disengaged. Use this feedback to refine your content and delivery. Once you've ironed out the kinks, record the course. Then, set it up on your chosen hosting platform, complete with a payment gateway. This approach ensures that your course is polished and ready for a wider audience, maximising its effectiveness and profitability.

So, run your course twice to get a feel for it, make adjustments, and then record it. By automating sales, you will free yourself from having to deliver it each time. Opting for a cohort model, where you interact with groups live, is a different approach but still worth considering. You might also think about offering two versions of your course: one live and one self-paced. This provides flexibility and caters to different learning preferences.

Stripe is an excellent tool for collecting payments. It deposits funds directly into your bank account without delay. While PayPal is popular, it can sometimes hold onto funds, especially if there's a sudden influx of orders, which they may flag as unusual. People have had thousands of dollars held back by PayPal under such circumstances. Stripe, on the other hand, processes payments smoothly and promptly, ensuring you get your money without hassle.

For advertising, I suggest enlisting an expert once you have solid sales copy that's converting well. Initially, you might want to run the course yourself, writing a few ads and setting up the landing page. Once these elements are functioning smoothly, an expert can fine-tune and perfect the ads to maximise your reach. Paid traffic guarantees sales because you can tweak your advertising and sales process.

Make sure you charge a reasonable course fee. Value your IP. You are giving people knowledge that they can't get anywhere else.

2. Running Coaching Programs

There are numerous ways to approach coaching, but the primary formats are one-on-one and group coaching. From a profitability standpoint, group coaching has significant advantages. Helping 10 or even 100 people at once, all paying the same fee, is a far more efficient use of your time. Group coaching also fosters a sense of community among participants. They often collaborate and support each other outside of your session – sharing experiences, tackling problems together, and learning from each other – transforming their learning into a team effort. These interactions help build strong bonds that sometimes last a lifetime, and importantly, this collective approach reduces the pressure on you to be the sole source of support and expertise.

When setting up coaching sessions, it's crucial to establish a clear time frame, such as one hour per week or one hour per month. Consistency is key. To make this work, you'll need a well-structured system. Use a mind map or a flowchart to outline the flow of your sessions, ensuring you cover all necessary topics efficiently. Schedule sessions for the same time and day each week or month. If you need to change the schedule for any reason, communicate this clearly to all participants. Let them know if you're rescheduling or recording the session for later viewing. This ensures that each session is productive and to the point.

Avoid trying to wing it, unless you have a set-up where participants bring specific issues and you provide on-the-spot advice. Having a clear plan will make your coaching more effective and ensure you consistently deliver value to your clients. This coaching style is quite different and involves setting guaranteed outcomes. It's essential to have a primary goal for the coaching program and a series of smaller, achievable outcomes. Ensuring that participants achieve these goals is crucial for their satisfaction and the program's credibility.

Remember that coaching is about helping people. Unlike a course, which is often a set recording of your teachings, coaching requires you to invest more of yourself. You'll be much closer to the people you're working with, answering personalised questions and providing tailored advice. This personal connection is a significant part of what makes coaching effective, but it also demands more from you. Be mindful of this commitment if you decide to pursue coaching. That said, coaching can be a straightforward way to build a profitable business.

Because coaching requires more of your personal knowledge and experience, you should charge a premium price for it.

3. Selling Templates

This idea is a bit different, but I have made hundreds of thousands of dollars from it. People are very willing to pay for ready-made templates for various software applications because it saves them time and the market is huge.

I once ran a website with 100,000 members who paid and signed up to download certificate templates. These templates were primarily for teachers, offering designs like "Best Student of the Day" or "Student of the Year". Teachers would download the templates, open them in Microsoft Word, customise them, and print them out for their classrooms. This turned out to be a very profitable business for quite some time.

Every day, people buy thousands of different templates for various applications such as spreadsheets, PowerPoint presentations, and WordPress websites. The range of templates you can create is vast and varied, making it a lucrative market to tap into. Whether for educational purposes, business presentations, or website designs, templates save time and provide structure, making them highly valuable to those who need quick, professional solutions without starting from scratch.

If you don't believe me, just visit ThemeForest and explore the vast array of website themes available for purchase. Or check out CodeCanyon to see the diverse range of code snippets and software templates on offer.

If you have expertise in a specific area, like crafting sales copy letters where users simply fill in the blanks, you can create templates for that. The possibilities are endless, and whether it's for websites, marketing materials, or business documents, the demand for well-designed templates is substantial. Take a look at Etsy and see the phenomenal range of templates available. If you're considering creating templates, focus on designing sets that help your audience improve or succeed by simply filling in the blanks.

When selling from the stage, ensure that your templates relate directly to your speech. This not only adds value to your presentation but also provides your audience with practical tools they can implement right away. Your audience should be able to download and use them immediately to enhance their business in line with your topic – anything from improving daily habits to building a better website. The key is to create templates that are easy to use.

Make sure to deliver your template packages electronically. There's no need to send physical copies. These templates are designed for use on computers, so keep the delivery simple and efficient. You can provide a link via email to a Google Drive zip file that customers can download. It doesn't need to be fancy; it just needs to be easy to access.

One of the most popular platforms right now is Canva. People are creating sets of Canva templates, which are particularly convenient. These sets often come as a single Canva file with, say, 50 pages, each page representing a separate template. This format allows users to access a variety of templates in one go, making it highly appealing and user-friendly.

For instance, I recently purchased a podcast promotion template on Canva, and all I had to do was fill in my own words. Canva is fantastic for this purpose. Leveraging Canva can be a game-changer for both creators and users. If you're considering diving into the template market, Canva is a platform you shouldn't overlook.

4. Daily Motivational Videos, Audios, or Tips

This is a great way to drip-feed content to your audience for a fee. Set up an autoresponder system that sends out a new tip to subscribers via email every day. You only need 365 of these tips, and then they can repeat annually, or you can add to them. This is especially effective with motivational content, as people often seek motivation at specific times of the year. You can tailor the messages around holidays, seasons, or any other themes relevant to your business.

You don't need to send out the actual audio or video files. Instead, host them on a platform like YouTube with the videos set to unlisted, so only those with the link can access them. Then, simply send the link to your subscribers. While video and audio can be impactful, text might be quicker to produce and easier to manage. You can efficiently create and send out daily motivational messages, ensuring that your audience stays engaged and inspired throughout the year.

Typing out text is quick for both you and your audience. It's easy for you to create, and people can read it quickly. Think about what would work best for you and your audience. If writing daily tips seems overwhelming, consider hiring someone to help with the writing. You can then record the tips or simply use the text as is.

You can charge a monthly fee, say $10, for subscribers to receive these daily motivational messages. This recurring revenue model can be quite profitable and provides consistent value to your audience. The key is to keep the content engaging and relevant to maintain subscriber interest and satisfaction.

At $10 a month, you're looking at $120 a year per subscriber. It's an appealing package due to its low cost and easy entry. There's no need for a hard sell – it's just $10, equivalent to a couple of cups of coffee, or even just one, these days. With 1,000 subscribers, you could be making $10,000 a month. That's significant income for sending out daily tips.

This model is proven and widely used. People love motivational content related to their interests.

5. Setting up Your Own School

Instead of offering one large course, consider selling multiple smaller courses as part of your own online school. This allows you to target specific areas within your expertise, creating a series of mini-courses. Each course should focus on one skill or topic, ensuring that participants achieve a clear and tangible outcome.

For example, if your field is business, you could have individual courses on effective marketing strategies, time management, financial planning, and so on. This approach not only broadens your appeal but also provides continuous learning opportunities for your audience. They can choose the areas they want to focus on, gradually building their knowledge and skills. This modular system can be very appealing, as it offers flexibility and a sense of progression for learners.

With this approach, your audience can select the specific mini-course that addresses their current business challenges. By offering a yearly membership, subscribers gain access to the entire library, enabling them to choose any course they need at any time. This not only adds value but also encourages continuous learning.

The beauty of a yearly membership is that as you gain more subscribers, you can continually add new content. This keeps your academy dynamic and ever-growing. You could name your platform something personal, like "Brad's Academy", or opt for a more business-oriented name, such as "Business Made Easy". You don't need to be an accredited institution to use terms like "academy" or "school". While there are certain regulations in some countries, for the most part, there's nothing stopping you from branding your domain as a business school.

Formalising your platform can add credibility, but it's not a necessity to get started. Simply buying a domain and branding it as your business school can be a powerful move. As you grow, you can always choose to formalise it further, but initially, the focus should be on providing valuable content and building your subscriber base.

Indeed, these are often referred to as non-accredited training programs. These aren't like official university courses but still provide valuable knowledge and skills in a particular area. As an expert, you can offer an unaccredited diploma in your field. There are countless examples of such diplomas out there, covering topics from life coaching to NLP and beyond. While some are accredited, many are not and are simply based on the creator's system and expertise. So, why not start your own school?

6. Creating an Evaluation Tool

This tool can be something businesses or individuals pay to access. One example I particularly like is the "Fascination Report". Users complete an online survey, and then they receive a personalised report that provides insights into their personality and how others perceive them. You can design a similar tool based on your expertise. This could help people learn more about themselves or their business, offering actionable insights for improvement.

For instance, if your expertise is in leadership, you could develop an evaluation tool that assesses leadership styles and provides recommendations for enhancement. Or, if your focus is on marketing, the tool could evaluate a company's current marketing strategies and offer tailored advice. The key is to create a valuable, insightful tool that aligns with your niche and provides tangible benefits to users.

Such tools can be a fantastic way to generate income while helping your audience achieve their goals. The reports generated from these evaluations can be detailed and comprehensive, providing users with a clear path for improvement.

Alternatively, you can resell existing evaluation tools with significant markups. For instance, 24x7assessments.com.au offers various assessments, including DISC profiles, at competitive prices. Lindsay Adams provides excellent pricing on DISC profiles. You might buy a package of 10 profiles for, say, $99 each and resell them for $200–$300 each.

Here's how it works: purchase the profiles, let the system generate the reports, and then work with your clients based on their results. This model allows you to make a good profit by adding value through personalised feedback sessions. For example, I know a business coach who charges $3,000 for a business evaluation. They use an existing assessment tool, then sit down with clients to discuss the results. Some business coaches charge even more. By marking up these tools and providing expert consultation, you can create a profitable revenue stream while offering valuable insights to your clients.

Evaluation tools can be highly profitable and provide a valuable service to your clients. Here's how to create and utilise them effectively:

1. **Develop your questionnaire:** Start by coming up with a set of questions relevant to your area of expertise. These should be designed to uncover specific strengths and weaknesses in your client's business or personal skills.

2. **Prepare the responses:** For each possible answer, write detailed responses. For instance, if a client selects option A, your response might be, "Option A indicates you need to focus on improving X, Y, and Z areas." Similarly, if they choose option B, your response could address different recommendations.

3. **Generate reports:** Once the questionnaire is completed, generate a report based on the client's answers. This report should provide a comprehensive analysis and actionable insights.

4. **Consultation sessions:** Sit down with your clients to discuss the results in detail. This personalised feedback session can be incredibly valuable and is often a precursor to selling additional services, such as business coaching.

5. **Custom programs:** Use the information gathered from the evaluation to create tailored programs or courses. For example, if the assessment reveals that a client needs help with digital marketing, you can offer a specific course or coaching package focused on that area.

By developing a robust evaluation tool, you can offer your clients precise insights into their business or personal development needs. This not only adds value to your service but also opens opportunities for additional revenue through personalised coaching or targeted courses.

7. Recurring Services

Recurring services are a goldmine. They offer a steady stream of income and provide essential services that clients are willing to pay for regularly. Here are some steps to implement this strategy:

1. Identify essential services: Determine which services or products in your field are indispensable to your clients. Think about services people need on an ongoing basis, such as bookkeeping, accounting, lawn care, pool cleaning, or digital marketing.

2. Create a subscription model: Develop a subscription-based

offering for these services. For example, if you're in digital marketing, offer monthly SEO maintenance, social media management, or email marketing campaigns.

3. Set up automated billing: Use a reliable payment gateway like Stripe or PayPal to automate the billing process. This ensures timely payments and reduces administrative work.

4. Offer value and consistency: Ensure that your recurring services consistently deliver value. This builds trust and loyalty, making clients less likely to cancel their subscriptions.

5. Market your services: Promote your recurring services to your existing and potential clients. Highlight the convenience and ongoing support they will receive.

6. Evaluate and improve: Regularly assess your services to ensure they meet client needs and make improvements based on feedback.

Recurring services are a win-win, providing clients with essential, ongoing support while generating predictable income for your business.

You can have a big set-up fee and then a maintenance charge, if you like. For example, you might charge $1,000 for an initial service and then $100 every month for ongoing maintenance. It's up to you how you set it up. One thing to keep in mind is that this approach requires commitment from the person buying from you. I recommend you sit down for 45 minutes with potential clients and sell to them directly. Talk to them, find out what their problems are, and then recommend the package that's best for them.

If you're in a service like lawn care, for instance, you might mow the lawns first and then discuss it afterward. Ask them questions like, "What else do you need doing?" or "Would you like your garden to look like this every month?" It just requires a little extra time to get to know the client to sell them into these sorts of ongoing services.

From a stage perspective, your goal is to sell the appointment. Basically, you're saying, "Hey, I'll sit down with you for nothing and see how I can help you." That's it. You talk about their business, discuss what you could do for them, and have a conversation.

This personalised approach can be very effective. By taking the time to understand their needs and showing how your services can meet those needs, you build trust and demonstrate value. This not only helps in securing the initial sale but also fosters a long-term relationship with the client, increasing the likelihood of recurring business.

What is the best option?

Recurring services are my #1 most profitable and leveraged product to sell.

Let's review all the options from the top:

1. Training courses
2. Coaching
3. Templates
4. Daily motivational videos, audios, or tips
5. Become your own school
6. Evaluation tools
7. Recurring services

This isn't necessarily the order I would put them in because everyone's circumstances are unique, and you need to consider what's best for you. There are many things you can profitably sell from the stage, but these are the ones I suggest you start with.

Take some time today to think about and plan what you could be doing next year to grow your speaking business. Set some specific goals related to products or services you can sell from the stage. Imagine if you could speak for free, get lots of gigs, build your profile, and have a product that sells itself. Realistically, what would that be worth to you over the next 10 years? $100,000 a year? $1 million a year? Honestly, it's totally possible if you plan it out strategically.

If you'd like someone to help you with this, I'm happy to assist. I coach people on how to build profitable businesses. Connect with me on LinkedIn, Facebook, or online. I'm not hard to find. I would love to chat with you about what you're trying to achieve.

Good luck in growing a massive business from the stage!

Brad

About Brad Hauck

Brad Hauck is a distinguished leader with over two decades of experience as a volunteer firefighter and a digital marketing expert. As the author of "Run Towards the Flames: Mastering Leadership in Times of Crisis," Brad shares his unique insights on resilience, adaptability, and strategic leadership. He hosts the "Profitable Speaking Podcast" and the "Leadership in the Line of Fire Podcast," where he blends practical business strategies with real-world firefighting experiences. Brad has helped countless businesses achieve top online rankings and navigate the digital landscape with agility. His compelling stories and actionable advice make him an inspiring voice in the world of business leadership.

www.firefighterbrad.com

Chapter 3:

Massive Media Coverage and Why It Matters

Kate Delaney — USA

Do you believe you have valuable relevant content, unique perspectives and the expertise to back it up? Tired of seeing people you think are behind the content curve getting a ton of media coverage? This is my charcuterie board of how to find the media, nail the pitch, get the coverage, and leverage it repeatedly.

Now more than ever, there are opportunities to land media for you and your business. As a media insider with two syndicated radio shows, I've landed coverage almost everywhere I speak. Most of the coverage has nothing to do with being a speaker or talk-radio host. Don't get me wrong; it doesn't hurt. However, it's the content, expertise and personality the producers want to use to fill the segments on television and radio shows. Provide great colour and context to written articles and you'll be quoted again and again.

Before we dig into tactics to serve up your irresistible pitches, let's make sure you know what's happening in the world. Do you avoid paying attention to what's making news because you think it is negative? You need to know what's going on locally, nationally and internationally if you want media coverage.

Being aware of what's happening is also one of the best ways to get heard on some sort of media. When there is breaking news, journalists scramble for different angles to add more depth to their coverage.

I have a crazy number of examples, but let's narrow it down. My friend Traci Brown, a certified speaking professional and member of the National Speakers Association, has accumulated a lot of media and hasn't spent a dime on publicists. She's been quoted in the *New York Post, Wall Street Journal, Huffington Post* – more publications than I have the space to mention here. NBC, CBS, Fox television and countless radio shows also reach out to Traci. Why? She's a body language expert with a personality and relevant interesting content. It didn't happen overnight. She developed her speaking niche and started going after media. By paying attention to the headlines, the culture, the stories, and then honing her unique spin, she started to get calls. Plus, she's a good guest.

Pay attention to what people around you are talking about. Is it taxes, real estate, money woes, health issues? On the lighter side, what should we stream that's worth binging? We are humans looking to connect. Look at social media to find out what's trending. What can you add to any discussion? Do you have a different take on what people are watching, listening to, or consuming? Then chase the media.

Let's head to what I call the "Parking Lot" for a second. Take out your phone, or a notebook –whatever works for you. Jot down everything you have some experience with or serious expertise in:

- Legal
- Business
- International travel

- Workplace culture
- Branding
- Communication
- Global remote work
- Starting a company
- Engaging employees in and out of the office
- Pop culture
- Diversity, equity and inclusion

Let's talk pitching and tactics. Know the media you are chasing. Make sure it's an audience you want to be in front of, and not one that doesn't work but just seems like a good idea. I've turned down some opportunities because I knew it wasn't a fit for me or them. Down the road when people are calling you, this still applies. Who do they appeal to? You need to know this so you can set up the proper hook.

Good Guests and Great Hooks

I was a television news anchor, and we worked on hooks or teasers half the day sometimes. You must carry an audience to the next segment. The number one thing the media wants is good guests with good hooks to reel in the audience. As speakers and trainers, it's the same thing. Pitching incredible titles with great content to meeting planners often makes the difference in whether you get the gig.

The hooks work for breaking information and some unique angle to pitch for a story suggestion.

Here are a couple of examples:

- Freaking out about the price of groceries and gas? Our next guest has five ways you can cut both in half, starting tomorrow.
- How to look like a million dollars for less than $50... That's coming up as we introduce you to an international speaker

willing to open their closet and share the secret.

What problems do you solve?

Zero in on the problems you solve. That's where the gold is in capturing media attention. We live in a *how-to* world. Show us something we never thought of or something we can't live without.

I've now interviewed more than 16,000 people. I've also worked in a mostly male-dominated industry. Here's what I want you to think about: What do you want to achieve with the help of media?

- Do you want to get heard?
- Do you want to get people to listen?
- Do you want to know how to fit in?
- Do you want to level the playing field?

There are more, but let's stop with those.

Golden Rules for an Effective Pitch

Your pitch should have whatever hook will get the editor, producer, talk host, or writer to click on your email right from the get-go. Put it in the subject line. Finding a number to text would be even better. More and more, text – not email – is the answer. It's fast in a busy world. If you position it correctly, you'll be surprised how many people will answer you back.

Another easy pitch is a tie-in with a time of year or event. What's coming up, and what can you tie into with your experience or expertise? My former client and friend Marco owns a series of pizza joints. He got major coverage during the Super Bowl. Why? Everyone talks about parties and ordering food. Pizza is the biggest seller. He has a great personality and is always willing to bring the product to the hungry radio and television people who asked him on the show. The American Pizza Community says 12.5 million were sold in the US in 2022. So many hooks here!

What's coming up and what can you tie into with your experience or expertise?

There are countless calendars of daily events. Comb through these as there seems to be a day for everything. Did you know that there's a clean comedy day? A zero–discrimination day? An international yoga day?

Some Affirmative Action – Your To-Do List

Let's go back to the Parking Lot. Do this today, or at least this week. In my experience, you might be saying these are great ideas. But somehow you never get around to following up on any of them. Believe me, I know. It happens to me all the time. We get bogged down in everything else we are working on, and forget to take a couple of steps that could land us some serious coverage.

1. Set up Google alerts and start following journalists, news organizations, publications, popular bloggers, radio shows and podcasters. Be aware of what's happening. Zero in on places, spaces and people to keep on top of it all.

2. Think locally, nationally and internationally. Make a list of places you'd like to be quoted or be asked to appear as a guest and pay attention to what they cover. Again, follow reporters, anchors and shows to get a better feel for the possibilities.

3. Once you get a call, text or email to be on the show or to send a quote to a publication, respond immediately.

Here's where too many people blow it. Nobody will wait for hours for you to get back to them. If you don't respond right away, that person seeking you out is reaching out to someone else.

What if you can't do the time slot or you're not available? Same thing. Let them know, and of course suggest they consider you for a future occasion. If you know someone else who would be great, recommend them. Trust me, it always comes back to you in ways you can't even imagine.

Being a Good Guest

Let's say you can make that TV appearance, send a quote, or jump on a radio show or podcast. Know their audience. Be yourself, but the best way to be invited back is to appeal to the audience and the interviewer.

Here's an easy example. If you are on a morning breakfast show that likes to let loose and have fun, make them laugh. Add funny stats or a story as it pertains to what you are talking about. Again, still be yourself. This would be different from being asked to provide some context about an ongoing crisis like power outages during a spell of extreme heat or cold.

Look at websites and, if possible, check what other guests they've had on. You'll have a better sense of what to expect. Surprise them! I was a regular on the BBC because of the way I compared American football to English football. It was fun and became lucrative as I eventually became a paid contributor.

Use something visual for TV or on Zoom. Lots of interviews are now done through Zoom. Can you think of a prop? Again, it all depends on the topic, but think outside the box.

A local television station in Dallas, Texas, wanted me to come on and talk about the Stanley Cup. I went out on a limb, but asked if I could have a scoring contest with the morning guy. I knew he was funny, and they were game. In the hallway of the TV studio, we set up a street hockey net and had a camera operator volunteer to be the goalkeeper. We shot Nerf balls at him with our sticks. It was fun, memorable and informative, as I still broke down the keys to winning the series.

Hall of Fame speaker Steve Spangler was the cool science teacher at an elementary school in Denver, Colorado. A local TV producer offered him a segment on the NBC affiliate. Think that helped him? You bet! He also ended up being the science guy on Ellen DeGeneres' syndicated television show for years. Look him up on YouTube to see all the traction. He's brilliant and was born for the success he's had because he really found his Wow. Sharing it on big media platforms only helped the brand.

Once you land a spot on something, don't keep it a secret. Get a copy of the show or publication you've been in and spread the word. Some people might frown on this and think you're bragging. To quote Hall of Fame speaker and massively sought-after consultant Alan Weiss, "If you're not going to toot your own horn, who else will?" I heard him say that at a breakout at one of the NSA Influence Conventions, and it has always stuck with me.

Social Media

This seems obvious, but link your media appearance to a post on Linked In or X, and put it on Meta, TikTok, Instagram or other social media. Thank the host, or mention something fun or funny behind the scenes. The key is to leverage the media across every form of media that you can think of – from everything mentioned above to your own website, newsletter or any place else that makes sense. Lots of speakers weave their media appearances into their speaker demos. Some use it on one sheet or as part of a video introduction. You never know who is looking or where they are looking, so leverage that appearance.

Here's something I am frequently asked by those in the speaking business: Am I really going to get booked from doing media? Is it worth the time? Well, that it's up to you. Not to go "woo-woo" on you, but I believe if it's planted in your head that anything you're doing is not worth your time, it won't be.

Why wouldn't it lead to those things for you if you have the right attitude? If you're being asked again and again to provide expert comment, be a guest and throw in your opinion, your media footprint grows. Do you think when event planners are looking for speakers, consultants, and trainers they aren't looking all over the place? I can track media appearances to meeting planners calling me to ask about keynotes. It's also led to more business for my VIP Experience workshops.

Yes, some companies and groups go to the same industry people from bureaus to agents to other speakers for recommendations. Thank goodness. But it certainly can't hurt. It just adds to what's unique about you. Why do speakers have a media tab on their websites or list the places they've appeared on their personal sites? It adds to the appeal.

Finally, I'll share the gentle reminder I have on my whiteboard in my studio. There are three circles: Desire, Action, and Consistency. The sweet spot where they intersect is coloured in. I'm confident that anyone who really wants massive media coverage and does at least half of what I have suggested here will get it. Imagine what it could lead to and how much fun it is to share your thoughts, ideas, and passions with another audience.

Kate

About Kate Delaney

Kate Delaney is a speaker, author, and Emmy Award-winning talk show host. Kate's interviewed over 16,000 people, including US presidents, Fortune 500 CEOs, and Hall of Fame athletes.

It took over 500 rejections, but she shattered the glass ceiling and became one of the first women to ever host a solo syndicated sports talk show. Kate's hosted shows on the NBC Sports Radio Network, the CBS Sports Radio Network and the number-one-rated station in the country WFAN in New York City.

Kate has most recently served as a keynote speaker and consultant for companies including Deloitte, Cisco, Exxon/Mobil, Stanley Oil and Gas, Forbes, UPS, Fox, AT&T, Kraft, Macy's, National Petroleum Energy Credit Association, NJ Credit Union League, Peach State Federal

Credit Union and many more. She also gave a TED-style talk at the Forbes Insider's Summit. Her keynotes and deeper-dive workshops are described as inspirational, engaging, funny and filled with actionable and implementable content.

She is the author of five books including her best-selling business book published by Forbes, *Deal Your Own Destiny: Increase your Odds, Win Big and Become Extraordinary.*

Kate is the past president of the National Speakers Association in Dallas, Texas. She is most proud of working with Children International®, helping several families in Ecuador, elsewhere around the world and in the United States.

Fun fact: Kate's an avid golfer, and brags about seven holes-in-one. Too bad they were all into a clown's mouth at a free mini-golf game. She lives in the Tampa Bay–St. Petersburg area in Florida with her husband, Paul, and golden retriever, Guinness, who never tires of chasing tennis balls.

www.katedelaneyspeaker.com

THE PLANNING

Chapter 4:

Harnessing AI for Writing, Planning, and Market Research

Dixie Carlton — New Zealand

I've been attending conferences for professional speakers for more than 20 years, and every time I hear the same messages: "Write a book'; 'Speakers with books get more bookings and higher fees"; 'A book is your best marketing tool.' It's true. I've heard it many times that unless you have a book, you may not even get a look-in. But I've also been at the front of the crowd saying that it's important to write and publish a quality book, because there are a lot of million-dollar speakers out there thumping desks with $10 business cards. Amazon and self-publishing technology has certainly made it easy for a lot of "desk thumpers" to swamp the marketplace.

In early 2023, the goalposts moved. Writing a quality book to help you market your business as a speaker changed dramatically once again.

Pre-2023, the idea of writing a book was always a good one, and you had various ways to do so without having to put in a great deal of effort into getting something useful for promoting your topic and you as the expert on that topic. There were ghost writers and book coaches in abundance to help with the planning and the process, and a growing number of people ready to charge you a lot of money to publish your book for you. That part has not changed. It's just become a lot more *interesting*.

Artificial Intelligence (AI) is transforming the landscape for non-fiction authors, particularly those who are also professional speakers. By leveraging AI tools, you can enhance your writing, streamline the editing process, and gain valuable insights into market trends and reader preferences. However, there are still drawbacks, and you still need to know how to use this technology well to not get caught up in a lot of quality issues and other turn-offs for readers.

Remember this: readers are becoming increasingly discerning about what they read or listen to, and how they want to access information. If you skip past this point, you'd better have a good lifejacket in order to swim with the experts now.

Let's explore how AI can help you maximize your potential to write and share great content across multiple platforms.

AI Tools for Writing and Editing

You can now use AI to simply enter a topic, have it create your plan, detail your highlights, identify specific bullet points or information, and train it to write in your own words. You can save money on editing, and even have your covers designed by AI now. But you need to humanize everything you do, and not just assume that your robot assistant will do a great job without being checked up on, *diligently*.

Overview of Popular AI Writing Assistants

AI writing assistants like Grammarly and ProWritingAid have

become essential tools for authors. These platforms offer advanced grammar and style checks, helping authors produce polished, error-free manuscripts. They have been available for a few years now and have continued to advance well in usability.

Grammarly:

- Provides real-time suggestions for grammar, punctuation, and style improvements.

- Enhances readability by offering recommendations to clarify and streamline text.

ProWritingAid:

- Analyses writing for grammar, style, and structural issues.

- Offers detailed reports on readability, overused words, and sentence variety.

Both tools help authors improve readability and coherence, making their manuscripts more engaging for readers. But they are not replacements for a human editor. Structural editing is critical for high-quality books and development of your highly engaging content.

Remember this, too: just as it is important for your audiences to not be turned off by too much wordage on a PowerPoint, or suffer death by numbers if you're talking about technical details, your stories are best not left to chance when working out which ones to share and how to fit them well into your content. **Stories make the facts sticky.** AI cannot write your stories for you. And that's an important point to consider. If you have great case studies or examples to demonstrate your expertise, then use those, and they are your stories to tell. So, *you* need to write them. This is one thing that always sets you apart from the clinical, robotic *(I don't care how clever it is),* manufactured content that AI produces. You would never let your PA present as you on stage, so don't let AI try to walk in your shoes when really it is best at just planning and accessorising your wardrobe.

Benefits of AI in Editing and Proofreading

AI-driven editing tools provide an additional layer of scrutiny, ensuring manuscripts, reports, and presentations are polished and professional.

Error detection:

- AI tools catch grammatical and typographical errors that might be overlooked during manual edits.

- They also provide consistency checks, ensuring uniformity in tone, style, and formatting throughout the manuscript.

Efficiency:

- Using AI for initial edits can save time, allowing you to focus on refining your content and addressing more complex issues. While this is also a big time-saver, you want to be sure of not having your own voice or specific jargon polished out of the final version.

If you want to develop a presentation based on a chapter, or a whole book, you can use AI to identify the parts that you want to use for one or another of those purposes and suggest enhancements, slides, handouts or worksheets based on the main content too.

Using AI for Content Generation and Idea Development

Now is a good time to bring Chat GPT into the discussion. When I talk about AI, I'm mostly referring to ChatGPT Open AI, which I use a lot as an author, coach, and publishing specialist. I use 4.0 – the paid version – and have trained it, ringfencing specific aspects of how I use it to ensure content I work with is not public or used to train other ChatGPT models. AI can assist in brainstorming, out-lining, and generating content, which is particularly useful for overcoming writer's block and enhancing creativity.

Brainstorming and outlining:

- I like to explore planning, structure, and even high-level branding aspects of a book or author profile by using AI in specific ways. If I put the right information in and guide the process with well-considered prompting, then I can usually get fantastic results that I can work with in much more straightforward ways.

Content Generation with ChatGPT:

- Tools like ChatGPT can create text based on user-provided prompts. This can be particularly useful for generating initial drafts or developing new ideas.

- ChatGPT can also help explore different angles and perspectives, adding depth to content and adding research options to work with too. One simple example is when you want to write different versions of your bio or introduction for one type of audience vs another, each featuring different aspects of your background or expertise. You can use your full biography and upload it for reworking ideas with the right prompts to ensure the variations you are seeking.

Disclaimer: I used ChatGPT to work out the various outlines and identify some of the content I wanted to use in this chapter. But this is still at least 80 per cent written by me, and this book is edited by a human editor and proofed by another real person too.

The Right Prompts

Prompting is something that you need to learn how to do, and there are a lot of brilliant tools and videos for doing so. If you don't get savvy with this, there is the very real risk of "garbage in, garbage out".

Let's say I want to write a good description for a workshop. These two examples show the differences in what I will get back:

- "Write a description for the workshop based on the attached document, which I can use to sell on my website."

- "Suggest appropriate keywords and then write a keyword-laden description for a workshop targeting HR management who are fighting with new laws and regulations about recruitment in the mining industry. Use the attached document to identify quotes and outcomes for those attending this event. The description will need to be 300 words long and will be used on a landing page for registration."

Which do you think will produce the better outcome?

From there, you can also prompt a specific sales letter, keywords and sales lines for use in social media posts, images for briefing a designer, and more. By the way, it does take practice to get it right and often several attempts to refine your prompts to get the exact outcomes you want, but for the time it saves in many instances, it's worth persevering.

AI for Market Research

AI tools can analyse market trends, reader preferences, and competitor performance, offering valuable insights that inform writing and marketing strategies. For example:

Analysing Market Trends and Reader/Audience Preferences

Understanding market trends and reader preferences is crucial for non-fiction authors. AI tools can identify what topics are in demand and how readers respond to different types of content.

Trending topics and popular genres:

- AI tools analyse large datasets to identify trending topics and popular genres, guiding you on what subjects to focus on, so you can tailor content to meet current market or industry demands.

Reviews and feedback:

- By analysing reader reviews, AI tools can highlight common themes and preferences, providing insights into what readers appreciate and what they criticize.
- This feedback helps authors refine their content to better meet audience expectations.

Specifically for Authors

AI can monitor competitor books, providing insights into their strengths and weaknesses. This information is invaluable for authors looking to position their books effectively.

Competitor monitoring:

- AI tools track the performance of competitor books, analysing factors such as sales, reviews, and rankings.
- Understanding what works for successful books in your genre will help you refine your strategies and differentiate your content.

Strategic insights:

- AI analysis of competitor books can inform decisions on topics, structure, and marketing approaches, helping authors create more competitive offerings.

Resource creation:

If you have a book you want readers to act on, so that you increase your chances of further engagement and additional speaking opportunities, then try asking ChatGPT to review your manuscript and create a few checklists, or a series of quotes you can offer as a downloadable resource. You can then have these on your website or on a reader landing page, in exchange for a sign-up to your database. From there, you can remarket to them about your speaking, coaching, training, or workshop events.

Audio Books and Podcasting

You have a book or two, you're getting some reasonable sales and a number of reviews, and you know that you get work as a speaker beyond the stage because of your marketing strategies with your book. Should you write another book, or diversify the content you already have?

Let's consider your options.

You might spend a lot of time writing and researching a new book, or you could revise your existing book(s). I'm always a fan of having at least two books, or more. The value in having a strong back catalogue cannot be overestimated in terms of marketing reach. If people like one book, they are highly likely to seek your other book(s) and read them, further cementing you as an authority in your field. But not everyone likes to read, and some people prefer to listen, or to have their content delivered in short shots such as podcasts, videos or blogs.

Diversifying how, when and where you further engage with your market means keeping a close eye on their trending preferences, but also working to your strengths. If you have a great voice for radio, then podcasting is ideal. If video is not a scary option for you, then vlogs and YouTube are better options. Short books that then serve as extracts in a series of content based on the main book is also a very good way to drip-feed and market your books. This is an excellent way to use Amazon. If you are producing a series of shorter books that are also available as audio books, then drip-feed the series so that you work the rankings out in your favour.

For example, if you have a book that is 40,000 words, and you want to take two or three extracts from it and modify the text enough to make it a variable reading experience – perhaps some new content or revised case studies – then turn each of those extracts into a short e-book of around 8,000–10,000 words. Launch the first one in, say, February at a price of US$2, then turn that into a free lead magnet when you launch the second one in April at $3, and use both the first and the second ones intermittently as free lead magnets going forward when you launch the third book or the main book at $10 for the e-book (and make the print book and the audio book available at full price, whatever that may be).

When you speak, you can also use those shorter extract e-books as giveaways, instead of giving away the full-size version. These can still be turned into print options and are also easier to take to an event because they are lighter to pack. For that same reason, they won't end up in hotel rooms after the conference because someone didn't have luggage space for the full-sized version.

As a non-fiction author who is also a professional speaker, you can enhance your productivity, improve the quality of your work, and gain a deeper understanding of your audience by integrating AI tools into your writing and market research processes. Embracing AI technology offers a competitive edge in the evolving landscape of authorship and expertise.

Dixie

About Dixie Carlton

Dixie Carlton is a prolific author and publishing specialist with over 20 years of experience in the professional speaking industry. As the CPO of Indie Experts Publishing and Author Services, Dixie has been a vocal advocate for the importance of writing and publishing high–quality books to enhance marketing efforts and establish expertise in the speaking industry. Her innovative approaches to brainstorming, content generation, and marketability have empowered hundreds of authors to improve their productivity, refine their work, and gain deeper insights into content curation and sharing. Dixie is a recognised specialist in the use of AI, publishing platforms such as Ingram Spark and Amazon, and countless marketing resources to transform the landscape for non-fiction authors.

www.dixiecarlton.com

Chapter 5:

Applying Aviation-Grade Rigour to Your Business

Dave Greenberg — New Zealand

Being Ready for the Next Worst Day of Your Life

We all have bad days. People have them. Organisations have them.

One day, you will have your worst day ever. If you're prepared and/or lucky, you will survive that day, and then, sometime in the future, you might have an even worse day.

I've witnessed thousands of people's worst days. I helped save someone's life when I was only 13 years old. I then spent years as a volunteer firefighter and emergency medical technician (EMT). From there, I went on to spend 25 years as a rescue helicopter crewman in New Zealand, during which time I wound up being part of nearly 4,000 missions. Most of the rescued people survived to see another day, but many did not.

Disasters come in all shapes and sizes.

A natural disaster, such as an earthquake or tsunami, can kill or displace thousands of people and destroy communities and organisations. In the USA, the Federal Emergency Management Agency (FEMA) found that over 40 per cent of small businesses did not reopen after a disaster, and, of those that did, only 29 per cent were still operating two years later.

A family member dying in a car crash or the family home burning to the ground can be an equally big disaster for the family involved, but it will go largely unnoticed outside of their family and friends.

Over the years, I've seen that being prepared and/or a bit lucky might be all that prevents your worst day from being your *last* day.

One of My Worst Days

While in the middle of a hike in mountainous bush country, a 47-year-old man suffered a heart attack. It was a cold winter's night with a bit of cloud and just enough moon and starlight to make a helicopter rescue possible.

As we descended to just above the treetops, Brian, our pilot, lost visual reference with the trees outside the helicopter. Suddenly, he was staring into a big dark hole, with nothing to tell him where we were in relation to the sky, the ground or the trees.

Dean, our paramedic, and I were using night vision goggles, which allowed us to see that we were flying backwards, in a nose-up attitude, barely missing the trees a few metres below us. We were seconds from a crash, and probably death, if Brian could not regain control.

Luckily, Brian was an experienced pilot who effortlessly switched to "instrument mode" and used the helicopter instruments to return us to straight and steady flight. At the same time, Dean and I calmly painted a verbal picture of what we could see around us. We could do this easily because we used these skills on every flight.

This was a perfect example of our team using all our skills, training, and available resources to achieve a good outcome (in this instance, saving our own lives). In aviation, this is called Crew Resource Management (CRM). In the corporate world, it is more commonly referred to as "essential", "core", or "soft" skills.

CRM is the magic behind any successful, high-performing team. During this rescue it allowed us to work as a team, communicate critical information clearly and effectively, problem-solve, and create robust situational awareness and common operating pictures. CRM allowed us all to contribute to solving the problem.

I have no doubt that our collective skills and a bit of luck prevented a crash that night.

I also do not doubt that we were able to use the CRM as well as we did because we used it on every flight. When things changed from Business As Usual (BAU) to a life-threatening situation, we did not need to switch from "BAU mode" to "Incident mode". We calmly and professionally handled the incident as part of BAU – using the same language, procedures and techniques we used on every flight, perhaps with a touch more urgency.

From Rescue Helicopters to the Pandemic Response

By the time I finished my rescue career in 2019, I had clocked up 4,200+ hours of flying time in a helicopter, coming out the other side relatively unscathed. However, I realised time and again in those years that this was due to the high standards and rigour of aviation. I thought my days of using CRM were behind me, but my aviation and CRM skills and the frameworks I had developed easily translated into small businesses in corporate and government environments.

Like most of you in early 2020, I found myself locked down at home, thanks to the COVID-19 pandemic. I was soon hired into the New Zealand Ministry of Health Emergency Management Team, and became part of the National COVID-19 Outbreak Response team.

After a career working at the tactical/operational level, I found myself meeting almost daily with the senior leaders of many government agencies, as well as the New Zealand prime minister and the COVID Cabinet. During my 27 months at the Ministry, I gained invaluable experience in better understanding the role of governance, their strategic thinking, and ensuring that their direction was implemented at the operational level.

Today, I use my years of experience to help organisations of any size navigate any incident, any crisis, on any given day.

How Aviation-Grade Rigour Can Transform Your Business as a Professional Speaker

In aviation, the pilot-in-command is ultimately responsible for the safe operation of the flight. However, an underlying premise of Crew Resource Management (CRM) is that everyone involved plays a critical role in ensuring safety, regardless of their position. This means anyone who senses any danger must speak up, ensuring no one unwittingly allows the pilot to lead them into a crash.

The same principles should apply to your speaking business, even if it's just you and a part-time assistant. As the CEO of your enterprise, you bear the ultimate responsibility for its success and stability. However, it is crucial that every team member, no matter their role, feels empowered to voice concerns if they identify potential risks.

Building a Strong Team Framework

Like a pilot-in-command, you must ensure that your business operations are safe and efficient. This involves fostering an environment where open communication and rigorous standards are the norm.

Four critical components of applying aviation-grade rigour to your business:

1. Empower your team: Just as CRM encourages every crew member to contribute to safety, ensure that your team members – everyone from your virtual assistant (VA) to your accountant – can speak up if they foresee any issues.

2. Define clear roles and responsibilities: Aviation differentiates between the pilot, co-pilot, and ground crew. You, as the CEO, might handle strategic direction, while your VA manages day-to-day tasks, and your accountant ensures financial health.

3. Effective governance: In aviation, governance involves setting strategic directions and risk parameters. In your business, establish clear goals and acceptable risk levels. Ensure everyone understands these parameters and works within them.

4. C-suite and operational teams: Even if you are a sole entrepreneur, think of your extended team (accountants, VAs, coaches) as your C-suite and operational teams. They help implement your strategic direction and ensure everything runs smoothly within set guidelines.

BAU, Incidents, and Crises

Ensuring you and your team know the difference between three specific areas of business-critical planning will help with your overall approach to putting plans into action if required.

Business as usual (BAU): Your daily operations should be streamlined to handle routine tasks efficiently. Your team should be trained to manage these without your constant oversight.

Incident management: Occasionally, problems will arise that are beyond the scope of BAU. An incident might require specific expertise or additional resources. For example, a technical issue with your website or a significant error in your financial records would be incidents needing attention but not disrupting the overall business flow.

Crisis management: Crises are rare, but severe, events that can significantly impact your business. These require immediate and intensive management. For instance, a data breach or a major public relations issue could be considered a crisis. Your crisis management plan should detail how to handle such events, ensuring continuity in other areas of your business.

Your business crisis planning needs to identify the different levels of BAU, Incident, and Crisis, and ensure that your plans are suited to the reality at any given time. For example, what you might have set in place to deal with the urgent replacement or cover of a cyber security issue will be completely different from a natural disaster or a break-in to your premises.

Applying Aviation-Grade Practices to Your Business

In my rescue helicopter days, every mission started as BAU. If something went wrong, our team was trained to handle it within our operational parameters. Similarly, in your business, daily operations should be managed as BAU, with clear protocols for incidents and crises.

For instance, if your business faces a significant issue like a major client withdrawal (an incident), your incident management plan would activate, involving your accountant for financial advice and your VA for client communication. In a crisis such as a legal issue threatening your business's existence, your crisis management team (perhaps including a lawyer and PR specialist) would take charge, while you focus on maintaining other business aspects.

By adopting aviation-grade rigour, you can ensure that your coaching or consulting business operates smoothly, with well-defined processes for handling routine tasks, incidents, and crises. This structured approach will not only enhance your business's resilience but also empower your team to contribute effectively to its success.

The Rigour of Aviation-Grade Frameworks

Today, I work with organisations to help them navigate their way through any incident, or crisis, on any given day. I empower their teams to translate the rigour of aviation precision, teamwork and decision-making into their organisation and teams. I do this through keynotes, workshops and scenario-based training.

This approach works equally well for the C-suite, middle managers, and frontline workers because it improves each team's capabilities by enhancing their essential skills. It teaches them teamwork and decision-making skills that are as sophisticated and effective as those used in aviation.

Applying these "aviation-grade" frameworks can improve a team's operations by making it more cohesive, responsive, and capable of making sound decisions quickly, especially in high-stakes or high-pressure situations. It is also an excellent way for teams at different levels of an organisation to find common ground and work together.

The Three Core Frameworks

- TRUSTED – the things that all high-performing teams need to trust and the qualities that individual team members need to be trusted. Essential skills are an important component of this framework.

- The SIZE-UP – six questions that enable a team to quickly assess a situation and determine whether it should be handled as Business As Usual or requires an incident and/or crisis management team response.

- The Rs of Resilience – the ability of people or things to recover from problems. My "Rs of Resilience" framework looks at the various components that make up organisational and personal resilience and demonstrates that being prepared for what might go wrong is essential for creating resilience.

These frameworks help any organisation of any size to develop the rigour of aviation precision, teamwork, and decision-making that makes flying the safest mode of transport available.

Let's take a helicopter view of these frameworks and how they can assist you.

TRUSTED Framework

Being part of a high-performing team means that you need to trust many things and be trusted by the rest of your team. This framework examines the various things I needed to trust before I would hang below a moving helicopter:

- T – my technical skills. I spent hundreds of hours learning, using and perfecting my technical skills, as did every other member of the team.

- R – our resources. The day I thought the helicopter would fall out of the sky, or my safety harness would not hold, would be a good day to stop flying!

- U – you, the person I stare at in the mirror each day. If the day came that I stopped trusting myself, I knew I would have to give up the job.

- S – our systems, or Standard Operating Procedures (SOPS), were robust and allowed us to work as a team.

- T – the team. We had to have enormous trust in each other to carry out our part of a mission. We didn't have to like each other or have anything to do with one another when we weren't working, but we needed to trust each other during the mission.

The last two letters, the 'E' and 'D', are how we became trusted by the other team members.

- E – essential skills. These invisible skills are the magic behind any high-performing team and critical to being trusted.

- D – Don't be a dick! My mother tried to teach me this golden rule, but she used nicer language than this. To be trusted, you need to be a team player and play nicely with others. You need empathy, compassion and integrity. End of story.

This framework applies to sports teams, rescue teams, sales teams and your team!

When I work with corporate teams, we work through each of the steps to figure out what is going right, or wrong, within a team. When we focus on communication within the team, decision-making, error trapping, critical thinking, leadership, situational awareness, creating a common operating picture, standard operating procedures, stress, fatigue, and workload management, the results are amazing!

The SIZE-UP Framework

When I began my first-responder career as a junior firefighter in New York City, one of the skills we learned was how to assess an emergency scene quickly and communicate key information to others. In the fire department, this was called a "size-up".

I have modified that size-up by creating a list of six questions which can be used to assess any situation and make decisions on how it is handled: as a BAU, an incident, or a crisis.

The six questions are:

1. What is the nature of the situation?

2. Who is leading our response?

3. What do we know to be facts?

4. What don't we know?

5. What do we want to understand, and when?

6. When do we need to act, and how?

Always remember that you do not need to understand everything to move to Question 6 and set priorities for your actions. In an emergency, it is usually better to take some action instead of waiting for "all" the information to come in.

Rings of Resilience

In New Zealand, our emergency management documentation discusses four Rs. I have expanded this list to include a few other Rs, which allow you to create personal and organisational resilience.

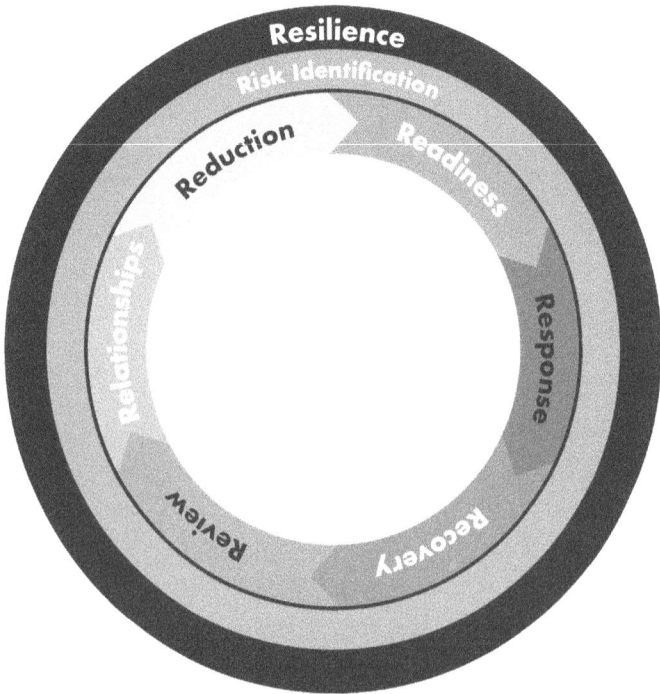

The inner ring is made up of six Rs:

1. Reduction – what can we do to reduce the effects of something that might go wrong one day?

2. Readiness – what can we do to be ready when that something does go wrong?

3. Response – what do we do when that something does go wrong?

4. Recovery – how do we recover and return to BAU (or the new BAU) after the event is over?

5. Relationships – what relationships do I need to establish before the event occurs, and which ones do I need to establish quickly during the response phase?

6. Review – what lessons do I need to identify, and what needs to be updated/ changed/implemented to ensure that the lessons were learned and the same mistakes don't happen again?

The ring outside these six is made up of Risk Identification, and the outermost ring is Resilience. When all those other things are in place, we create personal and organisational resilience.

Dave

About Dave Greenberg

Dave Greenberg focuses on empowering organisations of all sizes to leverage aviation-grade precision, teamwork, and decision-making for everyday operations and crisis situations. Please visit: www.davegreenberg.co/gss if you'd like to download some resources specifically for small businesses and a free e-copy of his book, Emergency Response: Life, Death and Helicopters.

www.davegreenberg.co

Chapter 6:

Crisis Recovery and Resilience

Bronwyn Reid — Australia

Planning to Survive and Then Thrive through the Big Hits

In early 2020, the world came to a grinding halt, and the conference and events industry worldwide shut down overnight, instantly putting every professional speaker's livelihood on hold. It was unprecedented and unpredictable, and no one was prepared for it. It's fair to say that while nobody can accurately tell what is ahead of us, even a small amount of thought and preparation can mean the difference between life and death for a business when a crisis hits.

In the dynamic world of professional speaking, the ability to adapt and thrive amidst disruptions is essential. The COVID-19 pandemic was a stark reminder of how quickly and drastically circumstances can change. As a professional speaker, your livelihood relies on your ability to connect with audiences, often through in-person events. When travel restrictions and conference cancellations occur, it can feel like the rug has been pulled out from under you. However, with thoughtful preparation and strategic planning, you can safeguard your business against such disruptions.

To meld my risk management knowledge and the framework I use for SMEs with some real-world experience for professional speakers, I turned to my #1 speaking mentor, Andrew Griffiths, and speaking superstar, Keith Abrahams. I am very fortunate to have had the opportunity to learn from both men, and to interview Andrew about his experience of the global pandemic.

Andrew told me that when he heard about the lockdowns, he was attending a conference in Adelaide, Australia, for (serendipitously) professional speakers. "There were 300 people in the room, and suddenly all their phones were going off at once. It was the sound of jobs being cancelled. Many people left that conference early to grab flights home, and panic ensued around the world."

Andrew estimates that, collectively, the attendees of just that one conference lost millions of dollars in professional speaking fees over the following two years.

While COVID-19 was the big one, there are many, many other traps out there for you as a professional speaker, just as there are for any business.

As an example, look through this list and consider whether one of these events would disrupt your speaking business – and potentially cause it to collapse:

- A long-term employee leaves and takes all their knowledge with them.

- A trusted employee commits fraud and steals tens of thousands of dollars.

- Hackers invade your computer systems and delete or steal all your files.

- You, or a family member, is injured, becomes ill, or dies.

- You go through a divorce or significant relationship catastrophe.

- Your best, and largest, customer decides to switch to another speaker.

- A new technological innovation suddenly makes your product or service obsolete (AI – voice cloning?)

Apart from the usual floods, fires, cyclones, divorces, cyber hacks, etc, there are some additional issues that professional speakers should consider:

1. Not being physically able to travel, speak, or communicate clearly.

2. Being cancelled! For a day, a week, or potentially longer.

3. Someone turning up in your space with exactly the same message – on the same stage.

4. Copyright infringement or investigation.

It's not much fun considering life and career longevity from the perspective of things going horribly wrong, but having some planning in place for the big "what ifs" really does help you to sleep at night.

Adapt, adapt, adapt!

Andrew observed that when COVID-19 hit, the professional speaking crowd split into two camps. First there was the "hunker down and ride it out" group. Many of them never came back. They became Uber drivers, or were seen sitting on street corners holding signs that read "Will speak for food."

The second group, many of whom are still professionally speaking, read the room and adapted – pronto. Keith Abraham took his credit card for a spin and purchased everything he needed to set up a professional home studio. If you've watched one of Keith's virtual presentations, you will know how impressive his set-up is. What speakers like Keith realized was that with all events going virtual, they had access to more speaking jobs worldwide without travel constraints. Andrew tells me he did paid presentations virtually in England, Spain, the US, South America, and Hong Kong. For my own part, I scored several gigs as MC of online safety conferences. That opportunity would almost certainly never have come my way unless someone was searching online for a professional speaker with a background in safety. Event organizers could broaden their talent pool.

When big things happen in any industry, and especially the experts, trainers, speakers and coaching industries, it not just about adapting to new technology. We need to have the emotional intelligence to assess whether our message is still relevant. When we were all struggling with COVID and what it meant, keynote presentations about "How to Maximize Your In-Person Networking Opportunities" would not fly.

Scanning the Horizon

Like an air traffic controller, part of your job is to continually scan the horizon – in your case, for trends that could affect you, your audience, and your business. My favourite approach is the good old PESTLE analysis, done regularly. You are looking for things in the following categories:

- Political
- Economic
- Social
- Technological
- Legal
- Environmental

It's a tried-and-tested framework to structure your search for potential hazards lurking in the shadows, waiting to disrupt your speaking career.

Being a Sole Operator

A professional speaker is a lone wolf. You can't employ someone to stand on the stage and speak in your place. So, a health issue can be a business-destroyer, and I have already mentioned the likelihood of this happening to any of us. This happened to Andrew when he was affected by Bell's Palsy – a critical condition for a speaker because you can't speak any more, or at least, speak as well as you could previously. I would like to quote an excerpt from our interview here, as it captures the terrifying reality of a business-ending event.

Andrew: *"When I had Bell's palsy, I literally lost feeling on one side of my face. There was no way I could speak, coach, or do what I do now. If it didn't get better, I didn't really have a plan for that. But I'll tell you what: sitting on the plane going back to Melbourne, unable to talk, I worked out my plan. Seriously, I asked myself, 'What will I do if it doesn't get better?' That was amazing, but it was also a grand learning experience. It gave me great power of empathy, understanding what it's like for people who can't communicate effectively. I'm a communicator, so my frustration was extraordinary. There was a lot of fear about my identity. If I was not a professional communicator, who was I?*

Me: *So, how did you get out of that?*

Andrew: *I took action! I realized that my greatest strength is my writing. I could still do that, and it would probably let me write more, and more effectively. So, I developed an intensive writing program. But then I was lucky; my Bell's palsy kind of cleared up in a month, with just a few residual things. But I tell you, my Bell's palsy rainy-day plan is never far away. My rainy-day plan is a double-sided A4 sheet covering about four or five different scenarios. I just sleep better at night knowing that if that happened, this is what I would do."*

The Jimmy Carr Problem

As a professional speaker, you are solely responsible for the words that come out of your mouth. And because you generally speak in public, those words hang around for a long time. Hence, they are always there, on record somewhere, with the potential to be unseated.

Comedian Jimmy Carr asserts that his career is already over. There is no doubt that somewhere, sometime over his career, he has said something politically incorrect that will come back to haunt him. He's just waiting for it to happen. "At some point, one of my jokes will become so unacceptable. At the moment it's fine, but I run the risk that someone will look back and go: 'He said what? It's over.'"

Ricky Gervais is one comedian who has famously decided that he doesn't care – and uses that to his advantage now. It's become part of his brand. He'll say "anything at all" and get away with it. But most of us don't want to test the boundaries like Jimmy, and most of us really do care that what we say matters. Still, the potential for a career-ending moment is always there, especially in this world of cancel culture.

Your Additional Responsibility

Thinking about the speaking industry, I propose that we, as professional speakers, have an added responsibility in a crisis – as if there isn't enough to think about already! I believe that as a voice of influence (that's why they pay you, right?), you also need to be the voice of calm and reason that your tribe/community/clients can rely upon. There are enough idiots following and regurgitating social media rubbish, indulging in self-aggrandisement, and being Chicken Little – the sky is falling. When people encounter a crisis, their brains freeze; they become incapable of making rational decisions.

You have a responsibility to stand above the crowd. Be a leader, and be part of the solution to the crisis, not the person throwing petrol on the fire.

Phone a friend

Your professional colleagues and steadfast friends are also a must-have. They will be there to help you pick up the pieces when the bad things happen. Just remember to reach out to them! For many in our industry, it was our colleagues and our ability to learn from each other that sustained us through the pandemic.

Again, being a sole operator means you don't have the same networks as a corporate inmate, but your network is there to share information, trends and updates – all helping you stay relevant.

So, while another business crisis is inevitable – be it something that is widespread or something that affects only you – the devastation left in its wake is not. I urge you to make this little bit of thinking and planning a priority. "It won't happen to me" is not a valid risk management plan, and a small amount of time spent planning now can save a world of pain later. Having the right support system is crucial. Knowing what could go wrong and having a plan is essential.

Any plan is better than no plan

One of the main themes of my book *Small Company, Big Crisis* is that having some planning is infinitely better than no planning. We humans react to shocks in one of three ways: fight, flight or freeze. We all know about the fight and flight – the adrenaline boost that allows us to escape a sabre-toothed cat roaming the plains. But the freeze is insidious, and potentially lethal. Your brain won't (can't?) make a rational decision – or even any decision at all. You are stuck, like the proverbial rabbit in the headlights, facing the oncoming disaster that's going to run you over.

Again, I quote Andrew Griffiths, who assures me he has faced his quota of business disasters. "For example, when I lost a big client, it was the attitude that was going to kill me, not the actual issue. I learned that not having a plan, the depression, and the my-business-is-going-to-end attitude was what would send me broke, not the actual issue."

The issue you face may not be one you planned for (I certainly didn't have global pandemic on my risk list), but a plan for any type of crisis can be adapted. Research showed that UK companies that had done any amount of risk management planning for Brexit survived Covid better than those who had not.

How do you start to plan for something going wrong?

Here's part of my six-step process to get you started. Take some time to really consider all the possibilities.

1. Think long and hard about what things could go wrong and impact your business. Divorce? Illness? Disability? Fraud? Bushfire, flood, or cyclone? Economic downturn? Pandemic?

2. Discuss how likely these things are to happen. Very likely, likely, rare...? For example, one in three Australian marriages ends in divorce, so one out of three of you need to prepare for the financial and emotional fallout. One in three of you will suffer a critical illness. One in 20 will suffer a total and permanent disability that will prevent you from continuing your career.

3. If one of those events does happen, what would the impact be? On yourself and on those around you? Who relies on you and your business?

4. How severe would that impact be? Would it be a mere inconvenience, or make you stop work for some time? Or stop you speaking at all, with a total loss of income and prospects?

5. Write down all the ways you could prevent the bad things happening. If they can't be prevented, discuss how you could lessen the impact, and write that down as well. I'm not able to tell you how to prevent a divorce, and you already know about protecting your health, so apart from seeking good insurance advice, you will have to work this out yourself.

6. Put all these preventative measures in place and review them

regularly. This is the step that is most often forgotten. Adapt, adapt, adapt.

Now FOUR things you can actively do when planning your next risk and recovery.

1. List all your assets; i.e., what additional skills you could harness and opportunities you might have if you need to pivot or earn an alternative income.

2. Check you are insured for all the things you can be insured for – including income, mortgage payments, illness, accident, death, trauma, loss of equipment, and professional liability.

3. Identify what needs to happen; i.e. who can step in and help immediately if something – anything – goes wrong, from missed flights, cancelled events, or accidents. Who will do what is necessary to keep the wheels turning or notify people immediately and keep them informed as needed?

4. Write your plan down and ensure your key people know where to find it and act on it.

It comes down to this. Having a plan, any plan, is crucial. Identifying potential risks and mapping out scenarios helps you sleep better at night. Planning for different scenarios, even simple ones, is essential.

It's not hard to figure out what could go wrong in our business. As speakers, we can easily identify potential issues like economic downturns, health issues, relevance of our topics, or something from the past coming back. Figuring out what could destroy our career and having plans for each scenario is critical.

Plan for the worst and hope for the best.

Bronwyn

About Brownyn Reid

Australian-based Bronwyn Reid speaks and coaches on The GAP Effect and helps large, medium, and small companies to resolve their limited understanding of each other's jargon and priorities in order to do better, bigger business together. The relationship between SMEs and their big counterparts (and government) is critical to economic success particularly where it impacts on supply chains. As the multi award-winning author of "Small Company Big Business", and "Small Company Big Crisis", Bronwyn recognizes that resilience and recovery planning are critical to any company's sustainability and has developed specific frameworks for teaching this.

www.bronwynreid.com.au

THE SERVICE

Chapter 7:

The Value and Rewards of Service

Lindsay Adams OAM — Australia

My journey began in 1998 when I joined the National Speakers Association of Australia (NSAA), now known as Professional Speakers Australia (PSA). At the time, I was a full-time employee in the Brisbane City Council and had a passion for speaking. My role in the Council involved presenting training seminars and workshops. I loved the power of the spoken word and the impact it had on others. As my passion for speaking grew, I became eager to grow a speaking business; however, I hadn't fully grasped the power of service yet. It wasn't until I attended my first PSA national convention in March 2000 that things started to click. At that event, I heard something that resonated deeply with me: "To grow your business, serve your chapter."

With this advice in mind, I returned home determined to act. I approached my chapter president, Cheryl Spicer, and asked, "What would you like me to do?"

"You used to work in the Tax Office, didn't you?" she responded.

"You can be treasurer!" And so that's what I did. I served as the treasurer and gave about a day or two each month to organising the registrations, collecting payments and sorting the name badges for the door. It was a small start, yet it was a significant step. I learned so much about the organisation and built strong relationships with my fellow leadership team in Queensland and the chapter members. Of course, being in charge of name tags meant I got to know who everyone was very quickly, and they came to know and recognise me too. Those leadership team members from my early days in this association are among some of my closest friends to this day.

> *"This initial act of service was the beginning of a journey that would profoundly shape my career."*

At the end of 2000, I attended the first national convention of the New Zealand National Speakers Association. It was there that I met David Price, a speaker from Perth, Australia. At the end of the last day of the convention, David and I and a couple of others stayed up into the wee hours of the morning talking about "all things speaking". David inspired me with this simple statement: "You know, you seem like a motivated kind of guy. You could be national president, even international president, one day." I was taken aback; his bold announcement burned an indelible mark on my brain.

I was one of Australia's fully trained business coaches, training with an organisation called CoachU. (This was before the explosion of the coaching industry as we know it now.) During my coaching training, the trainer said to me, "Sometimes you must set a vision for the client bigger than the one which they hold for themselves." David did just that.

Eventually, I became the Queensland Chapter President, and this put me on the national board. I was introduced to a wider circle of influencers within the organisation, and in a position to watch and learn from each of these legends within the speaking industry. The experience allowed me to develop leadership skills and deepen my connections within the association.

I was elected to National Junior Vice President (JVP), and that year I also served as the Convention Convenor. This role was a rite of passage, as the JVP was generally expected to organise the convention during their term. I served under the national president, Charles Kovess CSP, and we ran the event at the Marriott Hotel at Surfers Paradise on the Gold Coast in Queensland, where again, I could rub shoulders with some of the best local and international speakers. *My horizons expanded so much as a result of that huge project.*

I went on to become Senior Vice President and then President in 2006–2007. That was the year I received my Certified Speaking Professional (CSP) designation. I was now a working *professional* speaker.

Being National President was a transformative experience

I had the privilege of working with leading speakers from around Australia and the world. *It was a clear demonstration of how service can lead to unexpected and significant rewards.*

My journey didn't stop at the national level and soon my passion for service and leadership led me to the international stage. Toward the end of my term as national president in 2007, I figured I had one more year of service as immediate past president, and then I could hang up my boots. However other people had different ideas.

I received a phone call from Catherine Palin-Brinkworth one Saturday morning. She said, "I have a very important question to ask you. You will need to talk this over with your wife Debby before you can respond. If you were to be nominated for the role of international president, would you accept the nomination?"

I replied: "Oh, that's easy. We've talked about that! I never imagined for a moment that I would be considered for the role."

Catherine laughed and said, "Well, humour me. Please talk to Debby and let me know what she thinks."

I called Catherine back the next day to say we were in.

Of course, this process doesn't happen in a hurry. I was nominated and elected to the role of vice president of the Federation, which meant that I was in the line of succession to be president. I served two years, the first as vice president, then president elect. In 2009, I became the President of the International Federation for Professional Speakers, later to be known as the Global Speakers Federation (GSF).

This role allowed me to collaborate with a whole new level of influential speakers from diverse countries and backgrounds. Debby and I travelled to ten international events in that year of service, and the global perspective I gained was invaluable, providing new ideas and strategies that also helped grow my business further. Not only that, but I also made many new friendships and deepened existing relationships across the world.

These travels also opened business opportunities that I never dreamed of. One conversation turned into $100,000 worth of income in a joint venture with a UK-based speaker mate. Another adventure included an eight-course degustation meal with matching wines at a winery in the Niagara region of Canada – a meal I still have dreams about! I also earned a few frequent flyer miles, and I learned a hard lesson with regret.

At the end of that year, I contacted one of my existing clients, who informed me that while I was away, they had used the services of a competitor as they weren't sure if I was in the country. I was shocked that they could possibly do such a thing. I had believed they were intensely loyal to me and the services I provided. It was a hard lesson to learn and my fault entirely, as I had not kept in touch closely enough with my client base while I was off enjoying international travel. Make sure to take good care of your clients or they will quickly stray to other providers.

Beyond the Obvious Rewards

One of the most significant rewards of my service has been the extensive business and personal network I've built both locally and internationally over the years. Thanks to my involvement in PSA and the GSF, I can travel to any developed country and connect with like-minded friends and business colleagues. In fact, it's even better than that; I can stay in their house and be welcomed as a friend. This global network is a tremendous asset, both professionally and personally. The relationships I've cultivated continue to be a source of support, inspiration, and growth.

In fact, only yesterday, I was contacted by a dear speaker mate from South Africa, who was checking in to make sure we could spend time together in Bali at the Global Speakers Summit in September 2024 before, during or after the event, such is the level of connection between us.

One highlight of my career was attending the 2nd Annual Philippine Association of Professional Speakers (PAPS) Convention in 2018. It was at this event that I was inducted into the PAPS Speakers Hall of Fame. This came about from serving their association in their formation years, another unexpected delight and recognition from service.

In 2020, I was deeply honoured to be recognised in the Australia Day Honours for my service to the speaking industry both locally and internationally. Receiving the Medal of the Order of Australia (OAM) has enhanced my brand and brought new opportunities, further demonstrating the rewards of service.

The hard part about receiving this recognition was keeping quiet about it. It's a two-year process from nomination to receiving the award. In September 2019, I received an email from the Governor-General's office asking if I would accept the nomination. I hit "print" on the email and walked down to my wife's office at the other end of the house. Placing the printout in front of her, I asked, "Do you know anything about this?"

She said, "Oh, yeah, I've been meaning to tell you about that!" Unbeknownst to me, she had been supplying the person who nominated me with the necessary information. Now I had to sit on this news for another four months until the embargo was lifted and it could be made public. I told no one, not even my kids.

My story illustrates that the rewards of service are manifold. By dedicating myself to serving others, I've experienced significant professional growth. My roles in PSA and the GSF provided unparalleled opportunities to learn from industry leaders and apply innovative strategies to my business. The relationships I built during my tenure were instrumental in expanding my client base and enhancing my reputation.

Beyond professional success, service has brought me deep personal fulfilment. The connections I've made and the relationships I've nurtured are a source of immense joy and satisfaction. My journey has allowed me to travel the world, meet inspiring individuals, and make a meaningful impact on the speaking industry.

Service to Your Association

Have I inspired you to offer to serve your speaking chapter, or even other industry bodies you are part of?

Service is about giving of oneself to benefit others. Service is a powerful way to build relationships based on trust, respect, and mutual support. These relationships are not just valuable professionally; they also enrich our personal lives.

Service also fosters personal growth, challenging us all to step out of our comfort zones, develop new skills, and take on new responsibilities. My journey from a volunteer treasurer to the president of a global organisation is a testament to the personal growth that comes from service. Each role I took on provided new challenges and learning opportunities, helping me develop as a leader and as an individual.

Finally, service allows us to create a positive impact. Whether it's through volunteering, taking on leadership roles, or simply offering support to others, the act of service is a powerful force for good.

As you navigate your own career as a professional speaker, please remember the lessons from my journey: to grow, to serve, and to make a positive impact in whatever way you can. In doing so, you not only contribute to the betterment of communities you are part of, but there is a powerful ripple effect as we also enrich our own lives in immeasurable ways.

Lindsay

About Lindsay Adams OAM CSP

As the CEO of 24x7 Assessments and an award-winning conference speaker, Lindsay Adams specialises in understanding and bringing out the best in people. He has a wealth of experience in the assessment tool industry and has used thousands over the last 23 years in his own business. Today, he teaches others how to harness the power of these tools for quality outcomes with their people and stakeholders.

www.lindsayadams.com

www.assessments24x7.com.au

Chapter 8:

The Art of the Ask

Leila Kubesch — USA

How to Enlist Help from a Position of Power

One day, one of my 11th-grade students stayed back after class and opened up about his struggles. This conversation took place shortly after the lockdown in 2021, during a time when his parents had to work longer hours, leaving him responsible for looking after his much younger siblings. He mentioned that they had food at home, but he didn't know how to cook. His peers also shared similar experiences and expressed interest in learning. In response, I suggested conducting a cooking session over Zoom on a Saturday morning.

When the scheduled time arrived, many of the students forgot to log on. Some didn't have the necessary bakeware, and one student discovered that his dad had consumed all the eggs. As a result, the first lesson flopped. This meant I couldn't tackle this issue alone, and I needed to enlist help.

Asking for help is something I haven't always found it easy to do, and overcoming this tendency to "do it myself" has been a regular focus of personal development over the years. Valuing my time and my skills never came naturally to me. I have, however, come to recognize the high value in collaboration among like-minded thinkers and doers, and so I have developed a specific seven-step process for this.

My Seven-Step Method for Enlisting BIG Help

These steps must be used for each person or entity whose support you are enlisting.

1. Be specific about your goal.

2. Personalize.

3. Make just one ask.

4. Give a reason.

5. Give options.

6. Reciprocate.

7. Ease their minds.

Asking for a kitchen: I enlisted my school administrators to provide space to teach cooking after school, explaining that the project would meet a need for our students. To ease their mind, I added that I would volunteer my time and cover the cost of the food. All I was asking the school for was space, and they had the options of which space would fit the project. This personalized the request because they had the ultimate decision. Simple! Their answer was a resounding yes.

Asking for video production for the show: I approached the local cable television with a proposal to produce a cooking show we call "Chow & Tell", a teen cooking program, highlighting our project as part of their local programming to generate local interest and showcase positive initiatives in the community. The single request I made was for daily production, recognizing that this was a significant commitment. However, since they already cover programs daily and have the flexibility to edit at their convenience, it was feasible. In exchange for their production efforts, they were welcome to enjoy the meals we prepared during the show. They agreed to this arrangement, and we moved forward with the collaboration.

With any new initiatives, challenges will arise. The first meal was a disaster. The oven didn't work as we were attempting to roast two whole chickens. This motivated me to approach a local department store to ask for an electric range.

Here's how it evolved:

1. **State the goal:** "My students have expressed a strong desire to learn culinary skills, and I am offering to teach them through an after-school club focused on cooking basic recipes. The program, named 'Chow & Tell', involves preparing meals to share with their families and finding time to talk about their learning."

2. **Personalize:** "I am reaching out to you specifically because of your proximity to our school", (establishes a direct connection and convenience for collaboration).

3. **Make one ask:** "We require an electric range as open fires are prohibited in schools. Our request is solely for the range itself, without additional services such as delivery or installation."

4. **Give a reason:** "The motivation behind this initiative stems from the students' expressed need to learn cooking skills. With parents working longer hours post-lockdown, students have access to food but lack the knowledge to prepare meals."

5. **Give options:** "We are open to receiving a range in various conditions, such as returned, dented, floor model, used, or any colour available."

6. **Reciprocate:** "In return for your assistance, we can feature

your involvement in the local newspaper and on our social media platforms, extend an invitation for you to witness the program in action, provide a handwritten thank-you note, or offer other forms of appreciation."

7. **Ease their minds:** "We will handle the pick-up, installation, and any other necessary arrangements to ensure a seamless experience for you."

The range was delivered within three days, brand new in the box. Our district removed the broken one and installed within four days!

The program saw great success, with students eagerly staying after school to learn cooking skills. I went the extra mile by ordering aprons for the show, adding fresh flowers, and creating a welcoming environment.

However, as time went on, I began to feel overwhelmed. A full day of teaching in a mask followed by after-school activities took a toll. My routine involved teaching, assisting with cleanup, grocery shopping for the next day, and then starting the cycle again with my family at home. Furthermore, unlike a traditional cooking show where hosts are always made up, I often found myself wearing the same outfit without even realizing it.

To elevate the program and ease my workload, I decided to invite local celebrities to teach their favourite meals while I directed the program. I used the seven-step approach to invite the Superintendent of Public Instruction, who oversees all schools in Ohio. Initially, I attempted to contact him via email, but due to travel restrictions and remote work policies, he was unreachable. Knowing that he was an active user of social media, particularly on X (formerly Twitter), I reached out to him through that platform.

I followed the same structured approach I used with everyone else. For step 5, I presented him with options for the date of his appearance, ensuring it would be after school hours. In step 6, as a gesture of reciprocity, I offered him access to all the photos taken during the event. To ease his mind (step 7), I reassured him that all safety precautions would be taken, including masks for everyone involved, open windows, and the use of gloves.

I was ecstatic when he agreed to participate! Feeling inspired and grateful, I decided to elevate the event further by reaching out to a professional photographer. I explained which celebrity guest she would be capturing and proposed a collaboration: in exchange for her services, she would receive credit for her work through district social media, my personal platforms, and the guest's channels. To my delight, she agreed, offering her photography services free of charge.

With the photographer and celebrity, I was then further inspired to reach out to the local newspaper and share details about the program. The reporter came and featured the project, which garnered community support. The results of that meant I didn't need to pay for the food, and we even received grants to cover the cookware so the students could leave with the meal and everything they needed to cook it.

Thanks to the publicity from the newspaper feature, we received generous donations. These covered the cost of the food, and we even secured grants to provide the students with cookware. Now not only were they leaving with a meal, but they also had everything they needed to recreate it at home.

The Art of Reciprocity

Upon receiving the range, I felt compelled to express my gratitude, so I sent an email to convey my thanks and asked how they would like me to acknowledge their gift on social media. Their response was unexpected but heartwarming: "Please don't!" They shared that they were moved by the project and happy to contribute without seeking public recognition, as they were concerned about receiving numerous similar requests. This experience taught me that there are genuinely kind people who prefer to remain anonymous.

A few months later, when my fridge broke down, I could have easily purchased a replacement from a store near my location with a moderate discount. However, I insisted on buying it from the same store that had donated the range, despite the inconvenience. I wanted to show my appreciation and give back in my own way, even if it meant a bit more effort on my part.

Similarly, with the photographer, I took a proactive approach by writing a grant to hire her for a photoshoot featuring my students in a yoga session. Later, when I needed professional photographs for my website as a speaker, I naturally turned to her, further solidifying our connection and mutual support.

I never forget the kindness and look for ways to give back, even if not at the time it is rendered.

The MAGIC

I created an acronym for my students: Mastering the Art of Gratitude for Intentional Connection (MAGIC). I involve my students in this process through a series of three activities.

First, before the guest speaker arrives, I lead them to write thank-you cards and create a welcome banner.

The second part involves learning about the guest. For example, when a Muslim woman visited, they learned about cultural norms like not shaking hands with the opposite gender for greetings. Sharing this knowledge with the guests ensures prepardness and shows respect for their customs. The guests are always thrilled by the students' consideration.

The third part is crafting thoughtful questions for the event day. The questions must be unique, respectful, and show genuine curiosity. To enhance the guest's experience further, a student acts as an ambassador. They meet the guest and escort them to class, engaging in conversation along the way and ensuring they feel at ease. We end their time with us by presenting them with handmade cards.

The result is always magical for the guest. They express a desire to return, help again, and often mention having the best time during their visit.

How this impacts the professional speakers' industry

This is really about how we can impact our world through the recognition that we have a *duty of care* to inspire and make change. We are arguably more confident and reach more than many of our peers in the everyday world we live in, and it could be argued that without our taking an interest in community events, we are doing ourselves a disservice. We have supreme positions of strength because we are seen to be ideal spokespeople, advocates and supporters of those who do not have a voice themselves. We don't have to be "famous" to take a stand.

This is not about flaunting our talents but recognizing their potential value to others. Developing keen listening skills to understand others' needs and how they might benefit from our expertise is crucial. I've also found satisfaction in considering how I can empower others through my abilities.

As speakers, we can apply these strategies to enhance our personal lives as well. I've learned not to hesitate when seeking help from a position of strength. My powers lie in my skills and talents, which I can leverage to request assistance. This requires being a great listener, understanding what the other person needs, and finding ways I can help.

For instance, I utilized my photography skills to assist a professional speaker who needed photos on stage. This opportunity took me to Tennessee for my first paid gig, which was thrilling. It's amazing how simple acts of kindness and thoughtful gestures can create lasting connections and positive experiences for everyone involved.

During that time, speaker and author Steven Bollar *("Stand Tall Steve")* shared valuable insights about the speaking business. I captured stunning photos of him on stage and used the keywords to curate photos for his social media.

At one point during the photo shoot, I suggested a hike along the trails, but Steven hesitated due to his nice tennis shoes. Despite his initial protest, he ended up enjoying the photoshoot and appreciated the results. This experience taught me the power of leveraging my strengths to create mutually beneficial relationships.

The process

While I've honed many skills and earned multiple degrees, I initially relied heavily on training because I was hesitant to ask for direct assistance. I preferred investing in learning opportunities rather than reaching out for help. But mastering the art of working alone takes considerable time and effort. Through this journey, I've discovered that collaboration and seeking support not only lightens the load but also enriches the experience with diverse perspectives and shared expertise.

One effective strategy I've adopted is creating what I call an "Asset Menu". This menu lists hobbies, talents, and skills that I may not speak about but could leverage to assist others in exchange for help. This approach serves two purposes: it creates a boundary on my offerings and fosters reciprocity, opening a dialogue that maintains professional collaboration, mutual respect, and appreciation for the talents we bring. It's a reminder that we are not merely walking resumes, but we have other gifts beside what we do in our profession or speak about in our training and keynotes.

For example, my sewing skills go beyond creating garments; I use them to assist with wardrobe malfunctions on the go, costume design for the stage, and quick-change outfits, particularly useful in fast-paced situations. Regarding vegan cooking, my training in using food for healing allows me to offer rapid natural remedies for common issues like nausea, voice hoarseness, and body stiffness. My photography is aimed at capturing the artist within, be it a performer, speaker, or visual artist. Our needs are specific; we value photos that depict an engaged audience, capture our stage presence, or show attendees lining up to converse with us post-talk.

As you craft your Asset Menu, consider how your skills could benefit other speakers. I've learned that immediate exchanges aren't always possible. When the photographer generously volunteered her time for my students, I was deeply grateful but had no immediate way to reciprocate. All I could offer at the time was acknowledgment and a photo credit. However, when my students wanted senior photography, they went to her (she declined because it was not her specialty). Later, I used her services for all my photography on my own website. This approach is about *fostering a community* that supports each other for the greater good. We can create a professional community with mutually beneficial relationships, creating a network that knows the value of giving back.

Leila

About Leila Kubesch

Leila Kubesch epitomizes the transformative impact of community collaboration and strong family partnerships. Rising above challenges like budget cuts, her effort led to accolades such as Ohio Teacher of the Year in 2020 and National Family Teacher of the Year in 2021.

Renowned for her innovative methods and expertise in TESOL, Leila gives speeches that resonate globally, inspiring audiences and sparking transformative projects. Her approach, rooted in collaboration and gratitude, not only revolutionizes outcomes in the classroom but also propels her to remarkable personal success, earning her widespread recognition.

Through a captivating blend of storytelling, improv, and humour, Leila challenges audiences to embrace the power of support and join the 3 Cs movement – Communicate, Connect, and Collaborate – leaving a lasting impact wherever she goes. A graduate of Purdue University in Educational Administration and Indiana University in TESOL, she is a professional member of both the National Speakers Association (NSA) and the Professional Photographers of America (PPA), inseparable from her camera with a mission to give others a voice and visibility.

www.leilakubesch.com

Chapter 9:

Better Humaning. Better Business. Better World.

Brad Shorkend — South Africa

"The real danger is not that computers will begin to think like men, but that men will begin to think like computers." — Sydney J. Harris, American journalist for the Chicago Daily News.

If Harris was looking at us as a society right now, what might he be saying?

One of the prevailing mindsets of today's workplace economy is that humans are expendable, that the cost of their labour – and quite possibly their thinking – should be reduced or even eliminated wherever possible.

This mindset doesn't work!

The rules of humanity

Many organizations tend to forget about people being people...

still desiring, creating, and responding to human experiences. Even in this heavily digitalized age, humans are at the heart of business.

Simon Sinek, (New York Times best-selling author of Start with Why and The Infinite Game), says: "A hundred per cent of employees are people. A hundred per cent of customers are people. A hundred per cent of investors are people. If you don't understand people, you don't understand business."

Reading his words inspired me to build on them:

"If you don't care about people, you don't care about business."

We need to reconsider the way we think about this fast-emerging "next world of work" and to play the game of business as if people both inside and outside of our businesses matter more than ever. The lingering complexity of recent years has been how to more meaningfully connect with our people and access their next levels of ability.

Regardless of technology or the speed of innovation, people are still people and the rules of humanity still apply.

Yes, we are all going to have to "human" better, even more awesomely.

The companies and leaders who get this right are flourishing and will continue to achieve amazing results both at a transactional and at a cultural level. They understand that digital isn't something you do; it's something that you become while still making people matter.

They embrace the human factor; they "human" obsessively! In fact, they make "humaning awesomely" a non-negotiable part of their culture.

The speaking professional "unstaged"

So, what does this mean for those of us who have the privilege of earning our living as thought leaders, delivering our message and impact in various formats?

As speaking professionals, it is easy for us to fall into thinking

"I do my peopling from the stage." While this is true, it is only part of the truth. Yes, each of us has that thing we do that is productised, packaged and powerfully delivered to our audiences. And then, there is the entire other aspect of how we show up and the experiences we create in every other moment of engagement besides our on-stage activity. These are the critical human experience touchpoints of business.

Our businesses and our brands are about significantly more than just what we share in "stage mode", and this is where it becomes critical to expand our own awareness and our own "awakedness", our ability to be "switched on, tuned in, and adjusting to suit" (as written about in my book *We Are Still Human – And Work Shouldn't Suck!*)

Our entire approach to the journey that we speakers create for our clients and audiences is going to need to evolve to an even higher level of *humaning awesomely* – and to do this, we need a significantly better understanding of the current state of humanity.

It's all a bit of a mess.

Relational risk realities

Why do I say that it's all a bit of a mess?

The lightning-fast advancement of digital technology has gifted us with numerous obvious benefits such as increased access to information and multiple improved and convenient communication channels. That's fantastic, and necessary.

However, it has also led to a decline in face-to-face interactions and an increased sense of disconnection from other people. This disconnection (whether sensory or actual) is having severe consequences on the mental and emotional well-being of many people. In many cases, this disconnection is leading to increased loneliness.

The *mess* intensifies when digital communication leads to misunderstandings, misinterpretations, and an apparent lack of emotional intelligence, which can hinder effective communication and significantly damage relationships.

In a world where technology is increasingly dominant, it is even more crucial that we enthusiastically prioritize better "humaning".

We need to cultivate emotional intelligence, empathy, and compassion in our daily interactions. It's time to be wildly intentional about building stronger and more meaningful relationships and amplifying the level of care in the way we "human" with each other – and how we make each other feel.

This is the heart of the issue...

How we make other people feel is a skill

How we make people feel is a skill that does not necessarily come naturally. We may even take it for granted and assume that we are doing it well. As professional speakers, we might assume we have a better level of communication skills than most, but this is not necessarily so.

Collectively, we are not doing this well, and if we lose that distinct humanness and the ability to "human" well, then how different are we from machines when it comes to the experiences that we create?

Human vs Machine – and where humans win!

The most distinct difference between humans and machines lies in our capacity for perception, empathy, and emotional understanding.

Machines don't feel!

Machines don't care (or need to care) about the quality of the experience they create for another being, whether human or machine. Yes, I just referred to machines as beings... it can get very confusing at times.

While machines can process vast amounts of data and perform tasks with incredible efficiency, they lack the ability to perceive and understand the world the way humans do.

Even in a digital world, human beings are critical to shaping the future of business. Sure, machines deliver, but humans over-deliver.

Machines automate; humans innovate

Machines apply reason, while humans apply reason and emotion.

These subtle nuances can make the world of difference to the degree of relevance consumers assign to a brand and brand experience. There are certain human skills and behaviours that cannot (yet) be duplicated by machines. Curiosity, imagination and creativity are still very human attributes.

Machines cannot "people" better than people (will they ever?), and people cannot "machine" better than machines.

Humans are still winning in these areas of activity, but just doing is no longer good enough. We need to be continuously improving, and fast. Machines can gather and analyse data, but they do not possess the same level of perception as humans, and they do not have intuition or gut feelings. Humans can perceive and understand complex situations, including social and emotional cues which are essential for human interaction. Humans have the capacity to empathize with others, which involves understanding and sharing the emotional state of another.

This is a fundamental aspect of human social intelligence and is difficult (and, dare I say, impossible for now) to replicate in machines.

Machines can't understand and respond to human emotions in the same way that humans can. They are programmed to recognize certain cues but cannot truly comprehend the depth and complexity of human emotions. These differences highlight the unique aspects of human intelligence and the limitations of machine intelligence.

Up till now...

And then this happened...

GenAI (Generative AI) arrived in our reality, delivering two outputs that change the game.

Firstly, GenAI can engage in analytical and logical thinking (the human left-brain stuff), and secondly, at the same time it can also create almost anything that you ask it to across all platforms (multi-modal), which is likened to the human right-brain stuff.

When these two overlap, integrate, combine, connect, or however you might see them becoming mutual with each other, the AI can now start to interact with us humans with an elevated type of intelligence that can only be measured and viewed as even beyond human genius and, in many ways, even feel like human interaction.

Even more significant is that AI's intelligence is doubling every five to six months now, and that will get even faster. And it is getting even more "human" in the way it will engage.

Speaking human – being human – being relevant

The rapid advancement that I have described here is going to force us to find ways to go far beyond the *awesome* "humaning" that I casually mentioned earlier.

As speakers, what is going to be relevant to share with our audiences will be one thing, but the way we understand their worlds and create a complete experience for them from start to finish is where the rubber is really going to hit the road. We're going to have to "human" at a level that we may not have even imagined previously. It's where our relevance and our future success is going to be created.

Awesomeness is going to be essential.

To remain relevant, businesses must be very aware of, and very adaptable to, what is going on in the broader environment. This is where people come in, because people – not machines – have been and can (maybe?) remain the visionaries and the disruptors.

People notice, people intuit, people respond, people innovate.

What?... No, how!

The "what" is changing fast these days. If we obsess about it, then we will almost always be in the wrong place. We need to significantly improve our "how", the way we react and maintain the relevance of our responses to the present.

Again, better humaning.

For as long as we have existed on this planet, it's been about survival of the fittest. Long-term efficiencies. This is no longer true. It is now about the survival of the fastest. This mindset shift will require massive method adjustment, and along with that, a whole new set of muscles... to move from fittest to fastest.

How we do what we do will evolve, not only how we think.

James Clear, author of *New York Times* bestseller *Atomic Habits*, says, "*We don't rise to the level of our goals; we fall to the level of our systems.*"

I very much agree with this, but only if we apply a modern lens.

In the past, excellence equalled accurate repetition and duplication in pursuit of an objective. But this is like quicksand if we are repeating and duplicating systems that no longer meaningfully respond to the current state of humanity, business, technology, etc. It is not only a technological transformation, but also a conscious transformation – for those who get it. As human beings, we are having to evolve in terms of our own state of awareness and our own operating systems.

Without awareness, awesomeness is going to be a tough ask!

A Gentle Caution

While Generative AI offers us unprecedented advantages in crafting speaking content, when not "humanly" filtered, it also poses ethical considerations and challenges that demand careful and conscious navigation. Striking a balance between technological efficiency and ethical use is essential for responsible deployment and emphasizes the need for dynamic interplay between AI and human skills.

As GenAI continues to shape the future of professional speaking, deeper human intentionality will be instrumental in harnessing its potential while ensuring a harmonious integration with the human experience.

Transformation also comes loaded with an emotional obstacle course for people on the journey. There will be the anxiety of loss, and oftentimes sadness for having to let go of what we have been so familiar and comfortable with for so long.

There will be the awkwardness of the unknown "middle", the daunting space that we may find ourselves hovering in as we venture beyond our comfort zones to a new space of comfort.

We will have limited mindset, method or muscle to be highly functioning in this space as we find our feet there, but once we find our flow and become enthused by the possibilities ahead, we will emerge into a space with renewed excitement and meet the obstacles with openness and expansion.

And we will be tested to the core of our being and what we believe matters to us most and what we may define consciously or unconsciously as our values.

Our authenticity will be tested, as it is so humanly easy to revert to what used to make us comfortable.

And we must not! We need to dig deep, awesomely deep!

What are your rules of humanity going to be?

Mindset, method and muscle

What I have been describing here boils down to these three aspects: Mindset, Method and Muscle.

We can't run or hide away from the technological advances taking place, but we can evolve our thinking and mental frameworks around them. Without a Mindset reset or refresh, we are prone to wheel spinning in the same quicksand that we have been stuck in for years or even decades.

And if we don't get the base mindset right, then the behaviour that follows is, well, lesser quality "humaning".

For too long, we have made decisions from a mindset of protection, not expansion. When we start to think through a lens of "thrive" instead of a lens of "survive", awesome becomes possible.

The possibility opens up of evolving massively as humans, with and alongside technology.

The Method component would then be the systems and processes that give us the rigour and shared language to apply the Mindset we are implementing consistently.

The Muscle then refers to the skills and capability set required to do the work. This aspect is often overlooked. We all need to be in constant growth; our personal skills development project should be a constant – and relevant.

So now what?

I have been sharing here how I believe we can amplify our human awesomeness and, in doing so, how we can build incredible speaking businesses in an increasingly digital world.

We don't know what's coming next. How can we?

What we do know for sure, however, is that if we don't apply ourselves meaningfully to a higher level of "humaning", we are going be left behind.

And in the words of another client of mine, "It's not complicated; it's just hard."

We need to choose our hard.

Personally, I prefer the hard of getting out of my comfort zone in the interest of progress and awesome "humaning" – mostly on my own terms.

This feels way better to me than the hard of being stuck in my comfort zone while the world goes flying by – none of it on my terms at all.

I wish for you the courage of optimism, enthusiasm, and awesome humaning as you add your own magic to making the world an even better place.

Take care of yourself.

Take care of each other.

Human awesomely!

Brad

About Brad Shorkend

Brad Shorkend is a behavioural specialist and high-performance coach obsessed with helping businesses, leaders, and everyone who wakes up to go to work, to be better at the complicated job of being human.

Since 2005, he has worked with thousands of people around the world as a speaker and facilitator on how to better "human" at work, and in turn how to build and lead organisations that are awesome places for people to work at, to innovate meaningfully, and to deliver sustainable human success in a world that has gone digital crazy.

www.stillhuman.co.za/

Bonus Chapter

Presenting Your Author's Magic Wand

When speakers have books to sell at the back of the room, or to gift as part of their fees when presenting, the biggest challenge is often coordinating the printing, packaging and shipping of then to the conference or training event you are presenting at. You invariably have two choices:

1. Get books printed at your local printers, or in larger quantities in far off places such as China and India. This means storage, and often having a quantity that is unsold as you update your books over time.

2. Get your books printed in a guestimate quantity at the location where you are presenting and hope that the printer you chose to do this for you will get it right, deliver on time, and understand your specific files and instructions.

If electing the first option, that still means shipping them there, or even taking them as luggage to your destination.

Another option is to use a high-quality Print on Demand option, of which there are several from around the world to choose from now. However, many of these require a minimum quantity, and still end up being quite an expensive option on a per copy basis.

What if you could wave a magic wand?

Let's imagine this scenario:

The CEO of Fast Motor Group, Bill, wants you to present a keynote with a break out workshop over their three day event, with 150 delegates who all operate a city-wide dealership. Jack the person who is wanting to secure you for that date knows you have a book, and invites you to have some copies available, but please not to sell from the stage. This is a fairly typical situation.

You know that your book is of particular value and supports your keynote topic, and you also know that the budget for you as a speaker is part of one fund for the event, but that there are also likely funds for merchandising products for delegates.

Why not offer to have 150 copies of your book, signed by you, with an additional supporting message from their CEO on the inside first page.

It would read something like:

Dear Champion – that's the theme of this training event, because we're all aiming for the championship prize at the end of the conference – that being the trophy for who had the most success in the learning centres, and who had the most fun. I'm excited to be welcoming you to our grand event in 2025, and wish you the very best of all we have to offer you this week,

See you at the Opening Address,

Bill Windsor.

CEO
(Scanned signature)
(YOUR LOGO)

Then Bill tells you that he loves the idea of doing this, but could he see a sample.

You wave your magic wand, arrange a hard cover version with a jacket cover, personalised inside first page, and have it sent via Ingram Spark to arrive at his door within just a few days.

What happens next?

Bill calls you and asks to confirm the booking, and adds 150 books as discussed, and you just made an extra $2000 on top of your fee for the books.

But is that really possible? Yes, it certainly is. And Ingram Spark does this as a regular part of their service. From one copy, personalised for only $1 extra per copy, they can deliver high quality books directly to your destination. Maybe you only want 10 copies in hard cover for the VIPs in your training event? Maybe you want 500 copies all customised with a special back cover and logo.

Ingram Spark has been in the global business of printing and distribution of books for many years. Ingram Spark is not like Amazon – they don't sell directly to the consumer, but they do enable your readers to access your book in print and digital options from where they most love to buy their books. If you want your book expanded out to libraries and bookstores around the world, they can make it available to up to 45,000 outlets both online and in print.

As a professional speaker and member of the Global Speakers Federation, you are welcome to use the code for a discount off your next order anytime in 2025.

Please check out our Website, for more information.

www.ingramspark.com

indieXperts
PUBLISHING & AUTHOR SERVICES

We'll guide you through your entire Authority Journey

From *Pages to Stages*

- **Before** you write - development of a great manuscript,
- **During** the production and publishing process,
- **After** you publish - how to get leverage on your expertise.

EXPERTISE · SKILLS · BUSINESS

COACHING

CONTENT · SPEAKING · BOOKS

PUBLISHING

MARKETING

SOCIAL MEDIA · BRANDING

PROMOTION

Get your **FREE** personalised report - Are you ready to maximise your authority journey?

Take our quiz:

indieexpertspublishing.com

What non fiction authors really need to know about getting leverage on their authority.

Whether you're writing non-fiction e books, or selling your expertise as a writer of blogs and articles, the business of being a writer is exactly that, a business. It's a business for authors and experts who speak, retired professionals, people who have something to say and maybe want to change their corner of the world in some way. But what many authors don't realise is that once the book is written, then the hard work begins as you tackle the difference between being an author vs authority.

This book covers what you need to know including **file uploading, publishing options, social media, media training, planning your book and speaking professionally** about your topic. These are the things many authors are totally unaware of at the start of their writing and publishing journey, but are critical to the success of any book.

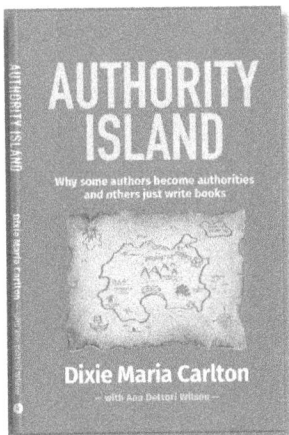

Access your FREE copy of Authority Island HERE

Register Early
GSS 2026

13–16 March 2026

Cairns Convention Centre
Queensland, Australia

SCAN ME

www.ingramcontent.com/pod-product-compliance
Lightning Source LLC
Chambersburg PA
CBHW040756220326
41597CB00029BB/4957